DREAMCATCHER

DREAMCATCHER
A Contemplation

Monika Singla

2024

Dreamcatcher: A Contemplation– published by Lithouse, Kashmere Gate, Delhi-110006.

© Author, 2024

http://ispck.org.in/books.php

ISBN: 978-81-19434-82-4

Cover Image: Adobe Stock/Pngtree

Cover Design: Anandita Singla

Laser typeset by

ISPCK, Post Box 1585, 1654, Madarsa Road, Kashmere Gate, Delhi-110006 • *Tel:* 23866323

e-mail: lithousehv@gmail.com
website: www.ispck.org.in

Printed at Saurabh Printers, Noida.

CONTENTS

CONTENTS

Acknowledgements

*L*ife's experiences and observations transpire thoughts that get scattered on the pages in the form of words. While treading this journey of transformation of words into this book I would like to cinch this opportunity to thank my publishers at ISPCK to make this manuscript a reality. My deep thanks to my editor Dr. Ella whose advice and kind words are always a pleasure to listen to.

My sincere gratitude to my parents and brothers for being a strong anchor in my life in this turbulent world and providing me with a clear vision. Blessings and love to Gulzar for being my *Boddhisattva*.

Thanks and love to my family for giving multiple reads to many drafts of my manuscript - my kids Anandita and Aditya, and my husband Sushil, where my thanks always begin and end.

Monika

ADVENT

Blaring speakers announcing the scheduled arrival and departure of trains, rumbling noise of engines, grinding sound of iron wheels on rail tracks...hubbub at the platform was imparting a frenzied flavour to the surroundings. The blending of all the sounds made them lose their meaning only to create a noise, numbing the mind. Every few minutes the space, which was the railway station got refilled with a new set of passengers, each exhibiting a different set of emotions. The only constants amidst this continual change were the hawkers and vendors ranting *chai chai* in their high-pitched voices, porters overloaded with luggage rushing hither thither...and the typical smell of the place. The aroma of eatables, the body odour of the crowd, the stench from the urinals and dustbins and the niff of smoke from rail engines- all merged into one, hitting the nostrils of every new entrant hard but also compromising enough to soon accommodate him in its embrace. Lowering of temperatures due to changes in weather was a breather, making these otherwise suffocating surroundings bearable.

Whether it is the months in a year or the years in age, they are all cognizable in the aspect that they lose their youthful vigour and ferocity as they progress. As the year ends, so does the steam of its youth- youth which it had flaunted in the form of sandy storms, extreme heats and colds, torrential rains- climatic extremities throughout, ultimately attaining the serenity and calmness of old age towards the year ending. This jilting of the poignancy of youth towards culmination, revealing the hidden mellowness underneath, sprinkles charm in the atmosphere making September and October the most cherished months. It is during this period that the extreme summer heat is neutralized by the stirring in of the right amount of coolness. It is then that the excess humidity of the monsoons is sucked in, and the dullness of the grey skies is wiped out, leaving behind a clear blue embracing the bright yellow of the sun like a jewel in the crown.

Equipoised nature is always alluring to both the restive and yielding minds alike, making these months the preferred time to satiate their cravings of wandering, travelling and delving deep into nature to rejuvenate themselves and overcome the weariness of their lives. It is at this time that people armed with their travel plans, their advance bookings for journeys to places they want to explore, of their sojourn, flood the stations. The aroma of the festivals around the corner and the coinciding wedding season add to the excitement of the salubrious and joyous environment.

Trains and buses running at full capacity, bus stands and railway stations bursting with the overflowing rush present a sight that would make any circumspect person think twice before jumping on the bandwagon. But Loveena did. And she did so without expecting anything from this journey, unaware of the fact that the outcome would be a grand one- one which only blessed souls can experience. But being the normal mortal being that she was, how could she have elucidated that without living through it?

To think...to analyze...to expect....are the attributes of the human mind, flaunted by it in an effort to declare itself the master of life- an illusion to which most of the earthly lives are confined. But what about those who have numbed their thoughts and have surrendered themselves to their lives...accepting their lives to be the master... they either are running away from this cruel master or had become immune to it...

And Loveena- which category did she belong to?

Was she running away or had become immune to the happenings of her life?

She herself was enveloped in a bubble of uncertainty...not only about the reason behind her presence amid that maddening crowd but about everything she could possibly think of. But this was not the proper moment to divulge into the depths of her life as she was trying hard to keep herself afloat at that time.

It was early in the morning someday in the first week of October that she had turned up at the railway station with her suitcase and a handbag. The shrill train horn accompanied by the grinding sound of its wheels on the tracks indicated its arrival, sending the crowd into a frenzy. Passengers with little children in tow and luggage tugging behind were running along the crawling train making even the normal act of boarding a train a gallantry task. In the blink of an eye, the entrance to every compartment was choked with passengers getting in and out simultaneously. Loveena, neither young enough to bear the push and shoves of the crowd nor old enough to earn empathy from the zealous passengers, felt her heart thumping hard against her chest, making her dread with fear at the very thought of getting through that crowd. This is the dilemma at this stage of life when youth is left behind, but old age is slightly far away to be embraced, that Loveena was passing through.

Fair complexioned, oval face decorated with dense ringlets of soft brown hairs like a halo, caramel-coloured eyes, dressed in an exquisitely crafted attire- reducing the age to nothing but a number for anyone who saw Loveena. The only evident indication of this number was her reading glasses dangling in a gold chain from her neck. Besides the snatching away of the sharpness of her vision the bad left knee, which gave away under the impact of any strenuous activity, was the only other sign that the passing years had marked her body with. This jerking bad knee had made her lose her balance on more occasions than once.

"It is always safe to steer away whenever you see a crowd... the collective mentality of a mob is unpredictable where every irrational act is hidden beneath the veil of anonymity." Her mother's reiterations since the time she herself could not recall had got embossed in her brain so deeply that whenever she saw a gathering, however small, these words would start drumming inside her head making her stressful and anxious. But her mother- she always was happy that she had cordoned off her daughter well from this *menacing* world without realizing that she had naively scraped her daughter of all the joys and pangs of growing up.

But now, with no choices to make, Loveena, despite her uneasiness, followed the porter carrying her luggage and became a part of the crowd standing in front of the compartment whose number was printed on her ticket.

Pushing and shoving is something contagious, affecting every person joining the crowd. So how could have Loveena been spared? With a strong wave of push arising from behind her, she entered... or more rightly was thrown into the compartment followed by the porter carrying her luggage.

"What's the use of getting educated if it fails to instil the basic etiquettes of behaviour in you?"

She directed her anger towards the bespectacled scholarly looking young boy behind her whose push had forced her in.

"Sorry madam. It's not me. I myself was pushed in by the crowd behind me," entering the compartment, he apologized. Ignoring him she threw a momentary contemptuous gaze at the unruly crowd and moved in to settle in her window seat. She had an aversion to crowds, to travelling and above all to using public transport.

     ADVENT

But now here she was – travelling in public transport amid that huge crowd.

When any task is undertaken, despite one's disliking, there must be some inevitable reason behind it. And there indeed was.

With all the disagreements she had developed not only with the people she had come in contact with but also with the circumstances that her life had posed her with, she had mastered the art of retracting herself from her surroundings, only to get immersed within. It was there that she had created an imaginary world that was always at her command, at her disposal- where she could travel down the memory lane or forward in time creating situations as she pleased. But now she found her inner self more chaotic than her surroundings casting shadows of doubt over the futility of her decision to undertake this long journey.

"Am I doing the right thing by going away from here?"

The boom of the abrupt squabble that erupted close to her, subdued the one that was going inside her making her notice her co-passenger- a fair complexioned, plump lady on the adjacent aisle seat- who was indulging in some argument with a man sitting behind them. Loveena swivelled in her seat to notice a medium-built man wiping his bald head with a handkerchief. The drops of water dripping down on that man from the wheels of a large red suitcase, which must have belonged to that plump lady, stacked on the overhead shelf by the porter was the culprit.

"Oh! Something is dripping down from your suitcase." Shouted the passenger to that lady.

"Don't worry. There's nothing inside it. The wheels got drenched in the water on the platform, it is that water that is dripping down from it."

This reply from the lady was more than enough to send that man into a fit of rage.

"What?" shrieked the man.

"*Bibiji*, my money. The train is going to start."

Unaffected by the ongoing squabble, the porter was getting anxious about his money.

The ongoing squabble, the anxious porter, the people standing or sitting in their seats, shifting restlessly...a glimpse of the madness that the whole world seemed to be engulfed in...and Loveena felt a fresh surge of confusion arising within.

Then the train whistled, and started with a jerk forcing the standing passengers to settle down in their seats.

With a smirked face Loveena slightly jerked her head in an effort to get herself disconnected from the surroundings, retracting into her shell.

The fair complexioned, plump lady undaunted by that squabble, after settling comfortably in her seat, pulled out a long box of chicken wrap from her big handbag that was lying in her lap. The white of her teeth shining like a string of pearls against her brightly painted lips pierced into chicken wrap taking out a mouthful of it.

Express trains are faster than passenger trains. And the speed with which every morsel was disappearing into her mouth resembled the stations passing by an express train- you just blink and you would miss the name of the station that passed by.

"Ah! What a voracious eater!" the thought crossed Loveena's mind.

Burrrp.

"...and superfast metabolism." A faint smile crossed her lips, and she closed her eyes.

"I should have waited some more time before making this decision?" As soon as she closed her eyes, she again got entangled in her confusion, arousing a fresh wave of restlessness.

Swoosh.

Loveena hibernating in her shell had failed to notice the bottle of Coca-Cola that the plump lady had pulled out from her handbag after finishing the wrap.

The vigour with which she had opened the lid of the bottle had led to a sudden spurt of the drink to spatter over Loveena's clothes. But before Loveena could understand anything, in a jiffy the lady pulled out tissues from that big bag dabbing it over the spill on Loveena's clothes.

"Sorry, sorry...."

"Oh! Please leave it, I will do it...." Getting irritated with the sudden turn of events, Loveena snatched the paper napkin from her co-passenger's hands. She felt as if the restlessness which she was running away from was following her like a shadow.

Whether it is the journeys *in life* or *of life* they have to reach their end point irrespective of the experiences endured by the traveller during that period.

The clickety-clack of the wheels along the rail track indicating the slowing down of the train resulted in the eruption of a sudden brouhaha in the compartment. The preponderance of passengers rushing to collect their luggage from overhead shelves, from underneath their seats, from the pockets in the seat covers or from wherever they had got a space to stow it away, created a sudden but anticipated chaos. This also indicated the finality of their long journey. *Pathankot* inscribed in bold black letters in English, Hindi and Punjabi was shining brightly against the yellow background of the approaching board, pillars, and projections of sheds leaving behind no doubt that the train had reached its final destination.

The fair-complexioned, plump woman was also struggling to bring down her big red suitcase from the shelf, while the man sitting behind them right under that suitcase was still snoring. She pulled and pulled and....there went the suitcase- coming out abruptly from the shelf, hitting the head of the snoring man with a bang setting the stage for a fresh round of squabble, with the man holding his head with one hand and wagging the finger of another one towards that woman.

And the woman...retaining the indifference of her behaviour, mumbled *sorry, sorry* and busied herself in adjusting the big red suitcase in the narrow passage in between, blocking it completely for the other passengers to pass through. Loveena kept on sitting motionless with her intent gaze transfixed on that suitcase. The spell of the moment made everything around her invisible, reducing that big suitcase into a big dot of bright red colour- an enigmatic colour having the power to unleash the temperamental bull hidden within passengers.

Boom.

And the bull got unleashed. An eruption of the fresh bout of altercation between the woman and the passengers brought her back to her senses. The woman unaffected by the squabble, soon busied herself in settling the fare with a porter who had entered the compartment as soon as the train touched the platform.

Crying infants, screaming children, anxious parents, arguing porters and passengers, a groaning man sitting behind....and Loveena, still grappling with her fears and confusions, this chaos was enough to numb her senses. She felt herself akin to a mute spectator observing everything around her with the least interest lamenting herself silently to be in such a place. *Ah! chaos and frenzy might be the only threads with which the matrix of the world is woven, entangling poor human beings into it like a spider* was the only recurring thought in her mind at that moment agitating her restless mind.

 ADVENT

Sitting under the influence of that intense feeling, the stillness in Loveena's composure showing no signs of hurry or excitement was complementing the touted sluggishness of the train. *Hurry, excitement*! There was a time when she also possessed those traits but that was *once upon a time* when she was a kid and that was a long, long time back. With only very few other passengers left to deboard she started attracting curious glances. Curiosity and question marks on the faces around her forced her to get up.

Pathankot being a troika of tourist places- Jammu, Chamba and Amritsar, was always overflowing with a rush of tourists. With churches from the Victorian era, famous religious places of Hindus and Sikhs and ruined forts of rulers from the bygone era- the city attracted both domestic and international tourists alike. But for Loveena, having no interest in travelling or...more precisely with no interest in anything...the place was just a dot on the map of the country. She, who in her life of nearly half a century had never travelled alone, cursed the moment from the day before when in a jiffy she had got her ticket booked and without any planning boarded the train.

It was her train journey that had ended, but not her journey.

The day had started to settle under the grey of the approaching night. She kept standing on the platform with her baggage, unable to decide whether to continue with her journey or to halt for the night. She knew that whenever she is in a spot her brain hibernated. She kept standing there waiting for that hibernation to be over and to get some response. Her further journey was a few more hours and was by road which she had not given a thought to. To give her journey a halt she needed some safe place to stay and that also she had not given a thought to. So, there were many things that she had not thought about but the things that she had thought about were also not sorted out and were still churning out confusion, making her more anxious.

She was in the middle of a journey the very purpose of which was unclear to her. The only thing clear to her at that time was that she was tired of life. So, was she running away *from* her life...or running away *with it*? If she was running away *with it,* then how could it be possible to get a respite at the place where she was going to? Tired of convincing herself, standing there on the platform with people rushing past her, she closed her eyes.

Loveena- with all the fears, anxieties and confusions...where was she heading to and for what?

LITTLE BIT OF HISTORY

"Loveena..."

On not getting sight of Loveena, Neena was getting jittery.

"Loveena..." running from one room to another in her search, Neena again called out her name in a tremulous voice. Immaculately stretched out bedsheets devoid of any wrinkle, properly arranged delicate perfume bottles and tiny cosmetic jars in captivating colours on the dressing table - everything was in perfect harmony with the placid stillness of the cozy bedroom, emanating a faint lime fragrance of the floor cleaner, thumpingly declaring little Loveena's absence. But despite that Neena, in an effort to assure herself peeped under the bed, behind the almirahs, beneath the folds of floor-length curtains... everywhere she thought of where a toddler could crawl to.

The undisturbed setup of the other bedroom and guest room added to Neena's anxiety. The resounding tick-tock of the clock, the only sound crushing the stillness of those passing moments, was hammering hard on her fearful heart draining her energy. The magnificent drawing room adorned with brilliantly shining crystals, teakwood furniture, antique pieces, and bright paintings adorning its spotless yellow walls, everything which had found its way into the house in the last ten years was also exhibiting an undisturbed splendour. But earlier also any of these things had rarely fascinated the little girl. Loveena, only a year old, still had a long way to go to perfect her walk. She, in her wobbly walk interspersed with crawling, used to criss-cross by all the things to reach some secluded corner of the house, where she sat silently with her gaze fixed on the fine line of ants moving along the wall or on some fly buzzing around her or sitting in the centre of the drawing room with her eyes fixed on the bright yellow dot formed on the marble floor by the reflection of sun's rays entering through large glass windows. Sometimes she stood in front of her mother's dressing table looking into her mirror image ignoring all the cosmetics lying in front of it. And the joy and happiness radiating from the little face was indescribable.

Throwing a cursory glance in the drawing room, Neena rushed out towards the staircase leading to the terrace. Overpowered by a strong feeling of terror she felt a sudden flush of heat pouring out from her body making her perspire profusely. Anticipating some untoward incident that might have happened to Loveena she felt her heart miss a beat and her vision got bleary with the stream of tears running down her cheeks.

"Oh, Loveena! Where are you?"

Running from one place to another in an agitated state she was muttering to herself. It was the first time in her life that she had cursed herself for having a colossal house which otherwise had always been a cynosure of her eyes. With everything-glossy marble floor, shimmering crystals, varnished and intricately carved teak wood furniture, splendid under the reflection of light entering in from the large glass windows were earlier the only things that she looked to for filling the voidness of her aching heart with a sense of accomplishment. But that was before Loveena's birth and now it was only the love of motherhood that occupied her soul squeezing out all other feelings into some distant corner of her heart making them insignificant. Now searching frantically for her daughter, the vastness of the house was baring her heart of all feelings except for fear and anxiety. It was her first encounter with those dreaded emotions since the birth of Loveena a year ago.

    LITTLE BIT OF HISTORY

...and the seeds of fear once planted were going to stay, to be nurtured and flourish by the love of motherhood. You love...you get anxious... you love more only to get more anxious, more fearful...and the vicious cycle goes on. Ah! And then the struggle starts to possess the source of love.

"Loveena..."

And there was she, sitting outside, with her little legs spread out in front of her, near a flower bed in their well-manicured lawn, staring intently at the multi-coloured petunias.

"Hmm...here you are."

Loveena raised her head and the depth and sparkle of her clear brown eyes lugged out Neena's fears enchanting them.

Neena smiled and Loveena giggled exposing her two small lower teeth, shining like milky white pearls.

Additions to the families are always earnestly desired and awaited. The moment in which this longing is relished is always cherished lifelong with fondness and is immortalized with its repetitive detailing till any of the parents exists. And so was Loveena's birth- the only one and that was also quite difficult. Her mother used to recall it so often, making every detail as vivid as possible that made her feel like going through the process again and again. Besides this it was also somewhat...or more precisely quite late in her parent's marriage – exactly after ten long years. In a society where parenthood is an essential component and is expected to be attained in the very first year of the marriage, ten years was the period sufficient for the *known ones* to label Neena with the title *barren*. *Barren* is not only derogatory for the women of society but also makes them misfits or more precisely unfortunate ones preventing them from attending auspicious rituals of the community.

Neena was also an outcast in the community. So Loveena's birth was the most awaited moment, a golden one, which Neena and her husband tried to engrave deeply into the rock-hard stillness of their lives by bestowing her with the most unique name they could think of- Loveena. It was a testimony to prove how unique and special she was in their lives, just like her name. Difficult was her birth but more difficult was her upbringing. It was not that Loveena was a difficult child but because of mollycoddling by her parents, especially her mother.

It is a belief that when a child is born his mind and heart are full of memories from a previous life. It is these sweet, bitter memories that make a newborn make faces or cry or giggle, even in sleep. But it was not so with Loveena. Most of the time when she was not sleeping, she was busy playing with herself, kicking her little legs and arms in the air, making gurgling sounds as if celebrating the joy of undertaking the grand journey of life. Always calm and at peace with herself. A God's child, a blessing. She either was a saint or must have discharged all her duties with perfection and detachment in her previous life. Only Loveena's soul would have known.

 Fair, chubby, slightly blond with big, brown eyes glinting with happiness and joy-a marvel of God's creation, created to be admired by anybody and everybody, making her mother put black threads around her neck, around her tiny wrists and feet and putting a black *tikka* on her small forehead. God himself might have felt anguish on Loveena's mother for marring the beauty He had created or ... might have cursed Himself for wasting his talent on carving out Loveena...or might have felt pity on Loveena's mother who was battling with her own fears of protecting her daughter from world's evil eye.

Hmm...Evil eye. But where is it?

      LITTLE BIT OF HISTORY

When life had served everything on a platter to Neena, ten years of wait to attain motherhood was the time when every passing year or year gone by deposited a layer of desperation in her heart which kept on transpiring in the form of fears from her every pore. And the cycle continued even after Loveena's birth. But now the shades have changed. Earlier the desperation was to attain motherhood and now it was for the well-being of her daughter... it was to protect her from the negative energies of the world... *but does the world with all its purity and beauty that one can ever imagine, could have evil eye or negative energy hidden beneath it... or that is hidden within every one of us, transpiring out slowly and slowly into the environment...making it toxic...making it fearful... fearful of ourselves, of our own thoughts.*

Neena's efforts to bring up her daughter with all the sagacity of life that she possessed started unfolding from the moment Loveena was handed over to her. Loveena's slightest whimper panicked her, and a sneeze was more than enough to rush her to a doctor. Her first step instead of arousing joy panicked her making her unroll quilts, mats and carpets all over the house to make little Loveena safe from even a scratch on her knees. Her first day in school was also Neena's first day of sitting on a bench in the courtyard of school... and that was not the last one. Loveena was out of her mother's womb a long time back but was still connected with some invisible cord, that never allowed her to grow independently. So nowhere was vacuity for anything else to flourish in Loveena's life other than her mother...and Babli.

GROWING UP

Contentment is a rarity among humans, whose absence is enough to create a void larger than even a black hole, and which thrives relentlessly by engulfing all the achievements and joys of life. Loveena's indifference towards the brilliance and captivation of materialistic accumulations could be attributed to contentment-the divine trait she was born with. The only other thing besides the beauty of nature that could hold her interest was her maternal grandparents' house in the small town of Bardha.

The enormity and grandeur of that massive structure had rightly earned it the name of a *haveli* in that small place. Being the only one of its types, it in itself was its own complete address. With the number of rooms exceeding the number that little child had learned to count at her kindergarten, unending corridors, archways, latticework, *jarokhas*-opening into a large central courtyard closed from the outside world, this *haveli* was a world in itself for the little child. As a toddler, she enjoyed holing up herself at any secluded place, which that massive structure had no dearth of. Crawling behind an ant only to poke her little finger into the hole it disappeared into, was one of the very few activities she kept herself indulged in most of the time. Indulgence in this trivial activity gave her immense joy that was exhibited in the gleam of her almond-shaped eyes and toothless grin.

How could a toddler evade getting distracted by the spotless brilliance of finely arranged crystal, from the garish-coloured toys scattered all around, from the snappy sound emitted by them...from everything and that too only to follow that small insignificant ant? Ah! Isn't she a fool of a little child were the only recurring thoughts in Neena's mind, amazing her.

The progression of infancy towards childhood led to the emergence of curiosities evoked by the grandeur of the *haveli*. With the scarcity of people living there, it being occupied only by Loveena's grandparents and their maidservants Rajjo and Bholi, the *haveli* was laced with an underlying sense of mystery that fascinated little Loveena. Her fascination accompanied by her childish stubbornness made her grandmother unlock those rooms which she herself rarely felt the need to even glance into. Little Loveena peeped into their darkness with widened eyes. Musty-smelling rooms filled with heavy furniture or with closed boxes or with trash, rooms with bundles of her grandfather's red bound *chopdis* (accounting books) emanating the strong scent of lignin.

The years adding to her age were adding to the curiosity of her inquisitive mind. And thus went Loveena forcing Bholi, her grandmother's maid, to open the dirt-laden boxes and yellowing faded pages of books... to scrutinize every nook and corner of those rooms very carefully. But all that she found were things of yesteryear...piles of small clothes, big used and unused clothes, toys...and whatnot from her mother's childhood. Not even one of those things interested her except for a big box, almost the size of a television, which Bholi told her was a radio that her grandmother had brought in her dowry.

"So much and too many old things you have piled up *naani*. Why?"

"Hmm...these are not just things but bundles of my memories."

"So, do you open up those boxes to visit your memories?"

It was, maybe for the first time, that little Loveena had created a memory regarding *memories- something stashed away into depths concealed safely from the world.*

Rajjo, take her away and tell her some stories were the only words that that poor old lady, puzzled by the depth of the question, could think of at that time.

You open boxes to visit your memories.

Rajjo took Loveena away leaving behind her old mistress with her thoughts raked up by her granddaughter's query.

The shallowness of human life all around was enough to dry up the bottomless well of joyfulness and inquisitiveness that Loveena was born with. The perpetuity of the process of drying up the divine trait left behind only confusion, fears, anxieties...

"Last night I heard a faint musical sound coming out of the room where that big radio is kept," Bholi said.

"Tell me more." Loveena's eyes widened with interest and fear.

"Sometimes you can hear footsteps in the corridors."

"Something more..."

And Bholi, filled with pleasure on getting such a response, kept on churning out more stories.

With time, all of Loveena's fascinations and curiosities evaporated, leaving behind fears and anxieties...which got settled in her thoughts...in her soul...in her eyes, forever.

With a child's body outgrowing her clothes, her mind also outgrows its fascinations quite fast. Loveena's interests also kept on shifting. With her fascination for the *haveli* now left behind, she developed an interest in knowing more about her grandparents.

Loveena's mother, Neena, a vivid recaller of her own childhood stories used to narrate about her life in that small town to Loveena. She told her how the growth of her father's stature surpassed the growth of that township, with him owning agricultural land, a petrol pump, a transport business and whatnot in that small place. The more he earned, the more he invested and the more he invested, the more he earned. Facing internment because of the limited opportunities in the place, he started investing in property at other places, thus expanding his empire. He expanded and expanded, touching the far-flung regions in neighbouring states and even the lesser-known places in the hills...but he merely touched them to create property.

Neena told and Loveena believed. Not only believed but experienced her grandfather's commanding position in the preferential treatment that she enjoyed wherever she went in Bardha.

But what Neena failed to tell her was that the more her father expanded, the greater a void was created within him only to be filled with desires for more and more, squeezing the relations, suffocating them. But relations are to be cherished, and not to be suffocated. Because if you suffocate them...they die. And with their end ceases the opportunity to learn and experience the diversity of emotions which is a prerequisite to pierce through the veil of earthly illusions and materialistic desires.

Loveena had one set of parents- Neena and Dev. Her mother and mother's stories were in every moment of her life carving out the person that she would become. *But where were her father Dev's?*

While blessing Neena's father wholeheartedly with materialistic bounties, God had acted miserly on the educational aspect. He was intelligent enough to understand the depths of business, to earn profits from his investments and then re-invest them, thus keeping him busy and submerged in the pleasures of the fathomless *samsara*. But despite all the comforts of life at his command, the only thing that made him feel helpless was his inability to understand the depth hidden beneath the words scattered on paper.

Maybe her father's yearning to fill this void led Dev's qualifications and job as an assistant professor of history at the university, project him as the most suitable boy for his daughter Neena. A friend of Neena's father told him about Dev and his docile nature – which her father felt to be another significant trait for his pampered daughter. So being an assistant professor became the only conspicuous thing in Dev's story making all other details insignificant.

Being the fourth one among a brigade of five siblings Dev's deprived childhood made him the man that he was- quiet, contented *or maybe indifferent*...with whatever ways life provided him with. Life was acceptable to him, and he was acceptable to life. Both co-existed peacefully without interfering in each other's ways. And he never interfered in the way of his marriage also. With Neena's parents always around her, filling her life with all the comforts she needed, leaving her with nothing to demand or discuss or argue about with her husband.... Moreover, Dev never resisted her in any matter. So Neena and Dev coexisted peacefully but without getting their stories ...or lives mingling with each other.

Most of the time even generosities of life test you. Instead of sinking silently into the ocean of life, they stir it and churn it. These very generosities stirred and churned Neena's life. Neena's possessions and her parents' status were enough to awe Dev's family.

Dev's parents had purchased their three-room house before his birth when they already were parents to three kids, not expecting the other two that followed. Years later, resembling the worn-out white terrazzo floor giving away its hold of the tiny pieces of chips,

                            GROWING UP

the elderly parents let go of their grown-up children to settle on their own, leaving behind only the eldest one and his family in that house. When Neena entered the house for the first time after her wedding it was overflowing...or apparently bursting with Dev's siblings and their families. Either it was because of the shyness of the new bride or the confusion of getting surrounded by that huge crowd of relatives that she kept her eyes down. Maybe for the first time in her life, she had seen so many feet tightly packed together obscuring even the floor underneath. Feet covered in flashy slippers, feet coated in bright nail paint, feet having chilblains, feet without slippers...so many people that she felt as if the front and rear walls of the house were forced apart only by the pressure exerted by them. The aroma of spices, smoke from the oil burning in a *kadhai*, steam from cookers whistling in the adjoining kitchen- everything mixing up with the body odour of that crowd was making that summer morning unbearable for Neena. She felt like opening all the doors and windows to get rid of that odour. But on her subsequent visits, she realized that that odour was a part and parcel of that house. It was woven into its texture; it's every nook and corner just like in most middle-class families having overused living spaces. Every middle-class family possesses a characteristic odour and Neena developed a *disliking for odours.*

Dev's family also accepted her into their family but without completely absorbing her into their lives like their other daughters-in-law. Her enormous wealthy background might have held them back from behaving normally with her.

There is only a very fine line between feeling respectful and getting terrorized. Dev's family had wiped off that line, thus mingling respect and terror together, making Neena's presence in the house uncomfortable for both parties. Neena- being a novice from an overprotective family with minimum relations to entangle into- failed to understand the reason for the coldness she experienced from her in-laws. Whatever little enthusiasm she had for gelling up with them soon lost steam, cocooning her in a shell. Whether it was her visit to her in-laws or the other way round, the atmosphere always tensed up with forced smiles plastered on their faces making them wish for quick passage of any time they had to spend together.

With the frittering away of time frittered away their relations... putting a quietus on them. Dev, who was the only connecting link between them, never tried to bridge that gap. Whether it was his indifference...or his fear of getting stamped as belonging to either the camp of his parents or his wife...or his anticipation of a war of words that could erupt with his interference...only Dev himself could have known. He never interfered. But this indifference earned him distance both from his family as well as his wife, leading to the casualty of *faith* in relations and birth of suspicions. This was to the extent that even when Loveena was born after a prolonged wait of ten years then was also an insignificant presence of Dev's family in celebrations.

So, Neena got married into that family without ever becoming a part of it. And Dev... either it was his detachment or lack of desire to recall the childhood that he had spent or any other reason he never weaved stories out of it.

Dev was always there but not his stories.

Deficient of trust in others, Neena's behaviour had always been profused with suspicions. Trust and faith are the traits of an uncorrupted soul so could be termed divine. Maybe it was the circumstances of her life that had bared her of these divine traits enabling her to pass them on to her daughter. Vexatious relations with in-laws, Dev's indifference and anguishing wait to attain motherhood were reasons sufficient enough to deposit innumerable layers of mistrust and suspicions in her mind making her believe in the premonitions that everyone ...or more rightly the world, with its uncertainties lurking everywhere, a perilous place to be in. And money, according to her, was the most powerful bait for attracting treacherous people.

Loveena, who was born with all Godly attributes-calm, pleasing, innocent, ever smiling, always eager to embrace everybody (even strangers) never earned approval for her behaviour from her mother. Neena always dismissed all these traits as incompatible with the ways of the world...a menacing place. With her deep-rooted thoughts and apprehensions regarding the menacing world, she was eager to weave the projection of her thoughts into the microcosm of the world that she was going to make around her daughter so as to entangle even her daughter Loveena into it.

Is it really true that He who is an eternal source of love, peace, and bliss could make a creation this menacing? Neena thought it to be so. And she might not be the only one in the world to think that way...thus getting fearful of His beautiful creation making life's journey a torturous one.

Love is an axle around which revolves around everything from the minuscule of human existence to the grandeur of the entire universe. It possesses the power to both mar and beautify the very essence of human existence. When it spreads around like an ocean, the existence of individual beings resembles the mighty waves arising and disappearing in that ocean. Every wave delving and celebrating the joy of being a part of that grand ocean. Arising from it fills the heart with joy whereas merger into it fills the soul with intense peace. But what happens when this powerful emotion of love instead of spreading out is focussed intensely and unidirectionally?... Then it resembles a tsunami giving birth to ferocious waves having the power to destroy everything that comes in its way. And they subside only to leave behind a trail of destruction, a void, a restlessness of the soul. And Neena's love for Loveena was like a tsunami-intense and unidirectional.

"We must teach Loveena the ways of life. Otherwise, people can trick her by exploiting her innocence."

"She shouldn't trust *everybody*. Not *everybody* but *anybody*."

Neena's love was worded most of the time in this monologue with herself.

Dev, true to his character, neither rejected nor accepted Neena's beliefs, so Neena self-accredited herself with the responsibility of resetting the traits Loveena was born with. And with this belief was laid down the foundation of Loveena's life whose attributes kept on oscillating like a pendulum between her natural and adscititious traits for the rest of her life.

Loveena got a family where the father is to be admired and the mother to be followed and have unquestionable faith in.

  GROWING UP

BABLI

*L*oveena, the child...and Loveena, the restless one standing at the railway station at Pathankot ...the in-between journey had very few witnesses and Babli was one of them.

There is a reason behind every presence in any house and so was behind Babli's in Loveena's house. Then that presence gave birth to Babli's story which got weaved with Loveena's.

The reason for Babli's presence in the household was Loveena or more appropriately Neena's fears about her daughter's safety. It was the day after that one incident when Neena had gotten weary of not finding Loveena in the house that Babli had been called for.

She was then a small, frail girl of eight or nine years. Her slight build was enough to indicate the deficiencies of life she had been enduring. When she appeared in their house for the first time with her mother Shakuntala, she was dressed up in a roughed-out salwar kameez and her thin hair was oiled and neatly but tightly plaited into pigtails clearly defining the facial contour of her small round face. Innocence and sincerity gleaming in her big, round eyes were too prominent to be ignored, making Neena hire her immediately. Her duty was to follow the little toddler like a shadow. She used to appear with the first ray of the sun before little Loveena could open her eyes only to vanish into the darkness of the night when Loveena fell asleep. Babli's persistent presence integrated her existence into Loveena's life to an extent where her disappearance for even a moment was enough to make Loveena restless.

"Bali...Bali...," Loveena babbled in her unclear speech.

Babli's mother Shakuntala already worked as a maid in Neena's house, doing household chores. She had been working for her since the time Neena got married and started her life with Dev in the government accommodation provided by the university on the campus. Within a few years, Dev and Neena shifted to their own newly constructed house in a nearby locality. Neena's address changed but not Shakuntala's. Shakuntala remained a constant in Neena's life.

Shakuntala belonged to that part of the society where males dominate the affairs of the family while the females struggle hard to make ends meet. Shakuntala worked and worked and worked... whereas her husband with no permanency in his work loitered around most of the time indulging either in skirmishes with the ruffians of the slums or in drinking or playing cards. A succinct description of Shakuntala's life was that it was screwed on all four sides.

Ten years...a decade is a sufficiently big block of time bringing out an appreciable change wherever it settles down. But Shankutala's lean and malnourished frame did not have enough space for this block to settle down, making it slip down over her. Ten long years... had slipped over Shakuntala like raindrops slipping down some wax-coated surface- without leaving any mark of its passing on Shakuntala.

Shakuntala and life always seemed to be at loggerheads with each other. Despite her hard labour, scarcity was deeply strewn in every aspect of her life. Life was adamant in not providing her with anything and Shakuntala also seemed to be adamant in extracting anything from that tattered life and while settling score with life she extracted children out of it. She gave birth to seven children, Babli being the eldest one.

                    BABLI

The baggage of poverty and six younger siblings made Babli quite mature for her age. With a single room filled to its brim with so many siblings, a drunkard father with a temper that could flare up at the drop of a hat and a mother worn out from the regular beatings of her husband and adversities of life, working in Loveena's house was nothing less than a pacifier for the little girl. Her world, which earlier was confined to the four walls of the room called her house, now expanded a little bit from that room in the slum to that palatial house in an elite locality. Loveena's innocence and Babli's maturity soon established a bond of love between the two. Babli followed her like a shadow all the time. Time, despite all the adjectives that could be attributed to it, the most undisputably eloquent one could be its fleeting nature. Every passing day, despite its monotonicity reflected its newness in emerging stability in Loveena's walk, clarity in her speech, joining of school and clearing of exams year after year to move on to higher levels and in her desire to widen the circumference of her world. But for Neena, the *world is not a good place to be explored* and Loveena obeyed. Loveena's world remained confined to the four walls of the palatial house. And Babli being a necessary ingredient was a constant feature in it.

"How could a person live in a place like this?"

This was the only thought that surfaced in Loveena's mind while climbing up the narrow and steep stairs of the dilapidated building that Babli lived in with her family. Shakuntala had rented a single room on the landing of the first floor with other rooms occupied by other families. Asking for Babli's room she glanced cursorily into rooms she was passing by only to find them overcrowded with children and adults... emanating an unbearable stench making her cover her nose with her handkerchief. And then she reached Babli's room only to find her lying down in a cot that was overcrowded by her siblings, busy shrieking, quarrelling, laughing. On seeing a young girl well dressed up in school uniform they suddenly hushed up.

Babli...

I am blessed to have a brick-and-mortar place to live in whereas many of my friends live in shanties which get occasionally flooded with rainwater during monsoons the oft-repeated words of Babli echoed in Loveena's ears.

This was the only time when Babli had been absent from Loveena's house for many days due to her illness and that was also the only time when Loveena had visited Babli's house to inquire about her well-being and also to satisfy her urge to see the place her *friend* lives in. *This was also the only time when Neena scolded her bitterly for this gesture of hers.*

''How dare you go anywhere without my knowledge?'' Neena shrieked.

And after that Loveena neither dared nor desired to visit the place.

Loveena was now a grown-up girl, but Babli still followed her like a shadow once she came back from her school. Both were flowing together in the stream of time exchanging stories from their respective worlds. Loveena told her about her day at school, her classmates and Babli told her about the notorieties of the ruffian boys in her slum, about the fights over a bucket of water or for using the common toilet which always had a long queue in front of it in mornings or about many other such things which made Loveena believe that the outside world was a bad place.

Whatever Neena said Loveena believed except that that she shouldn't trust Babli blindly as she was also a part of that bad world. With Loveena approaching her teenage years, Neena's fears were again changing the shade of their colours. At one time she had hired

Babli to get rid of the fears regarding the safety of her daughter and now Babli has become the source of her fears.... *she can spoil my daughter by telling her things from the slums.*

Shakuntala was bestowed with all the adversities but not with the time to brood over them, contrary to which Neena was provided with the delicacy of time served to her in the decorated platter of life. Time to brood over, to give birth to apprehensions and fears. And the fears transpiring from her every pore only mixed up in the environment all around her...suffocating her.

It was on the day Shakuntala told Neena about Babli's engagement with some distant relative of theirs that Neena was overjoyed. Babli got married leaving behind a void in Loveena's life but not without leaving behind a treasure trove of memories which would become one of the very few things which she would continue to cherish lifelong. With the strong beliefs passed on to her by her mother in an effort to protect her from the harshness of the world, she lost all interest in expanding her outer circle and the inner one- the relations at home started to contract with Babli's departure.

The slipping years were reflected only in the changing calendars on the wall, otherwise, everything else remained persistent. Every year started with wishing *Happy New Year* to the known ones, which amounted to a negligible number, making Loveena ponder about what happiness the new year could bring to them. The other constant was Shakuntala and Shakuntala's yearly demand for a hike in her monthly wage.

Life was moving slowly but smoothly ...but change is the law of nature.

AN UNEXPECTED UNFOLDING

The brightness of day gets overpowered by the darkness of night, the blazing heat of the summers gets bundled off only to give way to the shivering of winter, the dryness of hot weather offset by the dampness of rains, anthesis of dark green flower buds only to embrace the beauty of a flower and the flower turning into fruit and fruit silently changing its colour- everything provided by nature that a human mind could ever think of... is eager to change, eager to grow. How could life be exempted from following this trajectory? With its growth, life is liable to reveal its multifacetedness with the development of new relations and new emotions. Infanthood flourishing in the lap of motherhood tries to widen its horizon by embracing friendships of childhood furthering it with love interests of adolescence culminating in new relations of youth. The cycle of nature is the same with all its creations. Change...advancement... development... growth.

So was Loveena's.

Her engagement to Sanand was greeted as the most acceptable news by the known ones. Sanand, a well-qualified handsome young man from an affluent family, was considered to be one of the most eligible but unapproachable bachelors for middle-class parents with marriageable daughters. But with the beauty of a swan, character as unblemished as pure gold, riches of *Kuber*...and all the blessings that almighty can bestow one with, Loveena's engagement to Sanand was looked upon by everyone as something she rightly deserved.

Loveena's final year university exams were the only hindrance for her to get married. While Neena was not in favour of waiting for the exams to end, Dev wanted their daughter to complete her education. Neena was of the belief that marriage should be solemnized as early as possible after engagement but for the first time Dev objected to his wife's decision. And it was Dev who got away with his decision. Loveena and Sanand got a year of courtship where she was frequented by him. His visits became her most cherished moments to look forward to. With him, he brought her gifts. He was not the only one but also his mother, her would-be mother-in-law who kept on sending her expensive silks, bangles, jewellery, cosmetics...and whatever she could have ever thought of.

Loveena was making memories. But for Neena...the shades of her fears started changing their colour...she feared the aspect of a life being this perfect. How could life be so exquisitely crafted by Him? Adorned with all the colours of the rainbow. How could life shine with the brilliance of the sun without getting obscured by clouds? She feared that in the depths of the calmness of flowing waters disturbing currents may originate...she believed that nature never holds any prejudice. So how could life be an exception?

Whether it is the smoke of fears arising from within that starts reflecting in the happenings of life or it is the happenings of life that fan up the darkness of that smoke...a debatable thing sans climax.

Sanand's thoughts and her meetings with him were the only things to look forward to for Loveena. With her mind and thoughts fully engrossed in the dreams of the future, the lump in her leg was too small a thing to be noticed by her. It was only when it started emitting occasional pricking pain that it slightly attracted her attention. Neena applied poultices giving her temporary relief.

Neena felt her worst fears coming to life only to create obstacles in her daughter's life. At times, she felt guilty for giving birth to those fears. All her confusions, fears and forebodings that she silently endured amplified her anxieties culminating in her visits to priests and *tantriks* to get apotropaic magic performed by them. It was only when that lump started emitting excruciating pain, with Loveena finding it difficult to walk, that it came to Dev's notice. It was for the first time in her married life that Neena experienced Dev's outburst of anger on having been kept in the dark about his daughter's illness.

Neena's fears regarding the impact of her daughter's illness on her matrimonial prospects were also realized.

When Loveena was going through the physical trauma of undergoing scans and tests followed by surgery to get that lump removed, the mental agony caused by calling off the engagement by Sanand's family on the pretext of her illness was beyond her tolerance. She lamented. She cried.

This agony suffocated her, choking her soul, squeezing it off all the remnants of the traits she was born with. Her tears seemed to wash her soul of all joy and peace. All that was left behind were the smouldering memories of the time she had spent with Sanand. The smoke emerging from those memories choked her, making her restless.

She gasped for breath, for respite from that agony. But with the everlasting embers of agony being embedded deep within her, the respite was unattainable.

Resounding agonies of self are sufficient to extinguish all desires for worldly pleasures and are enough to make one believe that the *world is a difficult and menacing place to be in.*

Neena took this change as an indication of maturity- that her daughter had finally started to learn the ways of life.

...The rainbow of soul one is born with, replaced with the darkness of adscititious traits like the darkness of night and one is ready to face the world. And then the rest of life to be struggled through again to regain that lost rainbow...What an irony!

Illness and a called-off engagement were all considered misfortunes akin to defects in a person by Loveena's community, devaluing her matrimonial prospects. The elite class of society was not ready to make compromises by accepting such a girl into their family. While those with humble backgrounds were more than eager to accept Loveena for their sons *but ...Neena didn't like odours.*

Many times, Dev objected to Neena's mulish behaviour, but she remained adamant and Loveena- her memories with Sanand stashed away in her heart were not allowing her to make peace with anything else. Circumstances had completely moulded her into *Mama's girl.* The web of circumstances that life had weaved around them were tightening the noose around their necks making them desperate to break out from it.

Dev had scaled up his efforts to find some other suitable match for his daughter and Neena, she started consulting more astrologers, and holy and religious persons in an effort to ward off the evil eye - *of which she was always fearful.*

"Ma, stop doing this. None of these astrologers were able to predict my illness earlier then how can they predict my future now? Do you really believe in their dominion over destiny? Are they really powerful enough to alter the destiny a person is born with? So, stop finding reasons and solutions for them, from your *babas.*"

There always were those moments in a day when the heaviness of the situation became too unbearable for Loveena to contain in her heart, and all her frustrations vented out in the form of anger against all those *tantriks* and astrologers her mother was taking advice from in the hope of getting out from the muck of circumstances their lives were stuck in.

But for Dev and Neena, the desire to see their daughter happily married was the only driving force that kept them going.

Contemplations of the past only added exasperation to Loveena's behaviour, giving birth to an unease...to a disquiet which kept on accumulating within her. With the passage of time, these amassed frustrations and loneliness started forming a cocoon around her, severing all her connections not only with the outer world but also with her inner world- her soul, robbing her of *faith*.

And when this connection with the inner and outer energy is severed then life becomes rudderless and a painful journey. For Loveena that incident of the past proved to be the one which augmented her belief in Neena's words *that the world is a menacing place.*

She completed her education, took up a teaching assignment at university and kept the nothingness of her brain occupied by focusing on different aspects of her life. The more she focused, the more agitated she got.

The day she came to know about Sanand's marriage was the most devastating for her. When the whole world is ranting about population explosion, when the earth is falling short of accommodating people on its surface, then why was she snatched away from the only person she wanted to start her life with? *Why?*

And then what else could be more agitating than the question that in the warmth of their modest house on a cold winter morning, how did her father's heart suddenly stop beating- taking him from the present to past tense? This unexpected jolt of life clobbered up the remnants of Loveena's self, antecedently born with minimalistic relations.

     AN UNEXPECTED UNFOLDING

The debris left behind kept emitting dark smoke of fears, insecurities and anxieties.

Liberation is the ultimate end of every earthly existence...nature liberates its abundance, time liberates its moments, body liberates its soul...but circumstances make humans strongly hold on to and cling on to their belongings, and their relations, making them more possessive...And Loveena and Neena also clung more fiercely and more strongly to each other...

...And anything that's against the laws of nature is a source of worldly suffering.

Both Neena, who after Loveena's birth surmised her to be the axle of her life, and Dev for reasons best known to him only, never felt the need to expand their neglected social circle. But with Dev gone, bearing the gnawing emptiness of the big house had become a challenging task for the mother-daughter duo. So, Babli, once hired as a young girl to look after little Loveena was now hired again but now to look after an aging Neena and to get rid off the fretting emptiness of the house.

Only expansion of wisdom could be accredited with the real quintessence of growth because it is the only thing that has no constraints...no degeneration. Once attained, it is attained for eternity. Contrary to this, the growth in physical attributes has its limitations which after attaining a peak start declining. The buoyancy of youth which Babli's thin and frail build had exhibited in full vigour when she had left Neena's house to get married was now hauled away only to leave behind signs of aging besides blessing her with prudence, thus making her presence in the house a comforting one. She now was a mature woman having a treasure of her own worldly experiences to share.

She had left her work at their place to get married only to realize that her husband who worked as a daily wager in a factory was a drunkard just like her father. The deeply engraved impression she had of her father was that of him always being in an inebriated state whereas her husband used to be in that state for most of the time and not *all the time*. So, acceptance of his addiction came easy to her. Soon after her marriage, she started working as a maidservant in a nearby colony. This was the only way of life that she had learned from her mother and could follow. Her husband earned only to spend all his earnings on drinking. And Babli worked and earned money to spend her earnings feeding the family. She had accepted this arrangement without any qualms.

But sometimes or more aptly most of the time life wants to test the limits to which one can bear the adversities imposed by it without complaining. Only a few months had passed since her wedding when she was beaten by her husband for the first time, who was in a heavily inebriated state. But that was merely the beginning. She endured the beatings without any complaint and became a mother to his three sons. All her sons followed in their father's footsteps by submitting themselves to the allures of drinking at quite a tender age. But the threshold of all her endurances attained its climax when in a fit of rage, under the influence of liquor, she was beaten severely. It was not the first time that her husband had beaten her, but it was the first time that her sons had also joined him in this act. This incident left behind a trail of not only a severely injured body but also of tattered relations, forcing her to decide to leave her family and be on her own. She experienced the world only to turn away from it.

The grandness of the world makes the diminutiveness of human existence resounding, arousing the dreaded feeling of loneliness which Babli experienced at that moment for the first time. But the feeling was somewhat subdued by the fact that for her the world was confined to merely two places -one, where she was born and

                    AN UNEXPECTED UNFOLDING

brought up and the other where she went after her marriage. Her birthplace had lost its significance for her a long time back when she had lost the last of her parents. After all, the significance of a place is only because of the relations thriving there. With the loss of relations that significance is also lost. So, with the loss of her parents was lost the significance of the place where she was born, and where she belonged to. Her mother Shakuntala and her father Baloo had both died a few years back. Shakuntala to her old age and her husband Baloo to an accident caused in his inebriated state. Thus, putting Babli and her siblings on their respective journeys of their lives. But now with no interest in staying at her husband's place and having no parents to turn to, she felt the emptiness of a vast desert in her life devoid of anything comforting to cling to. The reminiscence of her childhood at Loveena's house jolted her out of that forlornness.

Babli's needs were very few, for shelter and food, which were fulfilled in Neena's house who in turn took care of Neena and the household chores. Hmm...*and the outer bad world superimposed perfectly over Neena's world. Is there really a good world and bad world...or merely one world...one and the only world all around?*

The house with three ladies, on different stages of life's journey, had also seemed to lose the stiffness of its youth. The brilliance of crystal and antiques was now hidden under thick layers of dust, teakwood furniture had started giving glimpses of wood after chipping off of its polish and the smoothness of marble floor was marred by fine scratches resembling wrinkles settled on once taut and youthful skin. Once spotless curtains with crisp pleats tied by beautiful tassels, which resembled the veil of a woman held up giving a glimpse of beauty beneath, were now sloppy with grease and dirt. It was either the despondency of the souls of people living there that was reflected in the shattering of the house or the other way round, the crumbling house reflecting in the shattering of their souls. But unfaltering was the fact that both were shattering, crumbling, shredding bits of their pieces daily.

Life comes in one size fit for all without any freedom to alter it. The only way to make it *wearable* or *bearable* is by adapting to it accordingly. Year after year it slipped like the grains of sand. The three ladies had also adapted themselves to the ways of life they were provided with. The emptiness which was still there became a part of their lives but when it got superimposed with the one created with the passing away of Neena, it became unbearable and engulfed Loveena's whole existence like a black hole.

A day's journey begins with dawn blooming into morning subsequently attaining the youth visible in the brilliance of the afternoon sun which mellows down into the softness of the orange in the evenings only to be obscured by the darkness of the night. Loveena felt a likeness of this journey to that of her biological clock. The only difference lay in the fact that unlike life every new day revives itself. With her embracing the forties, the brilliance of her youth mellowed down into the softness of the approaching old age. The unbearable silence and abundance of time scattered all around her played havoc with her senses, numbing them. It was the embers of restlessness and the haunting silence of her life that fuelled her desire for a family.

It had been almost four years now since Loveena had lost her mother, the last of her parents. Loveena married, not to start a family but to be a part of one and to drown the haunting hollowness of her soul into the joys and laughter of life. She married Vikram, one of her colleagues. The only thing she knew about him was that he was a divorcee with two grown-up kids. She married only to be a part of that family. His children living in his custody were regularly visited by their mother. It didn't take her long to understand that

     AN UNEXPECTED UNFOLDING

her position in the house was like that of an intruder. The more she tried to blend in with their lives, the more her efforts got negated. It made her realize the lack of anything in common between them to share, thus projecting her as akin to a stranger among them. Loveena, grieving her being left alone in the world without any relations to entangle with, soon developed a lot of conflicts with Vikram who was also badly entangled in his own relations, without being able to comprehend any way to sort them out. While at her mother's house, the hollowness of the surroundings perfectly overlapped with that of her soul, at Vikram's house the chaos of her relations was always at loggerhead with the hollowness of her soul, exacerbating the restlessness and anxieties which she was running away from. And all her efforts to replenish the barrenness of her life failed.

Vikram's first marriage was solemnized while he was still studying in college. At that time, his parents instead of consulting had merely informed him about their decision to get him married to the girl they had chosen. He, either due to timidness or shyness, failed to contradict them and performed all the rituals with disinterest. With a resentment clouding his senses, he passed through all ceremonies of his own marriage like a stranger. The marriage was solemnized with pomp with every arrangement meticulous enough to earn the praise of everyone except the groom. While Vikram was envied for this by his contemporaries, he himself was fuming from the inside liking himself to a sacrificial goat. The girl was pleasant and educated, the marriage ceremony was good, and everybody enjoyed- it seemed that life was quite eager to bless Vikram with happiness but...

...but had that happened, wouldn't everything become perfect in his life? So, the fumes of agitation arising from within him obscured everything that life was going to bless him with, leaving behind

the restless person that he became. He took life as a battle and the world as a battleground where happiness was a thing to be battled for. Ah! Delusions of the overworked human mind. He made his life a battlefield.

And so, he spent the next fifteen years battling against his self-created illusions without bothering about that girl- his wife. He directed all his frustration towards her by hurling abuses at her and by doing everything he could to humiliate her. After getting divorced from her and getting married to another restless soul he was still battling for the happiness and peace of mind that he himself had given up at the altar of his ego.

How could people like Vikram, whose own life had always been chaotic and directionless provide succour to another restless soul?

Life's nothing less than a kaleidoscope, where broken desires, relations and heartaches give insights into variegated aspects of human nature. But these insights are a prerequisite to get over the hangover of worldly desires and to see the eternal beauty of the world hidden beneath.

SEARCH FOR SOLITUDE

It was two days back that to get respite from the heebie-jeebies of life Loveena had got her train ticket booked only to board the train early that morning. Parting goodbyes, last-moment hugs with a promise of coming back, waving hands...by evoking a feeling of belongingness are enough to establish an emotional bond with the place. And their absence...Hmm! That makes departure easy but also makes the emptiness of life more resounding, more thumping which Loveena, despite the clamour at the platform, was experiencing.

She had had a pampered childhood, a relaxed and joyful adolescence which gave way to a youth laced with dreams of quixotic quests which nearing their realization came tumbling down with the unanticipated turn of events. It was in the disquietude of that situation that her yearning for belongingness was to such an extreme that forced her to get married. She married but only to alleviate her anxieties. The cocoon of her loneliness which she wanted to get rid of only hardened. Getting bogged down by her circumstances, she felt as if she had tasted enough flavours from the simmering pot of life and now was left with nothing more to learn or experience from, summarizing the world to be a hopeless place.

Banikhet, a small town submerged in the piercing silence of hills, had never been able to charm her. But it was a place close to her mother's heart who used to cajole Loveena to accompany her to Banikhet. Now pushed by the weariness of life, she was left with no choice but to head to that very place in search of solitude.

Self... obsession with which entangles one in worldly pleasures, only to smear that Self with the dust of agonies. And when these agonies start overweighing that Self, only then does arise in it the obsession for understanding that Self.

To own a house in the hills had always been considered a sign of sophistication, a luxury to be able to escape from the scorching summer heat of the northern plains. Above all, it was an expression of the riches that a person possesses.

It was the expression of her grandfather's riches. Or more rightly his compulsion for investment, that Loveena's grandfather purchased a property in Orchard Street of Banikhet. But he only invested his money and not his time in that property, because money was the only thing he had an abundance of.

To earn and *to invest were the* only things he enjoyed doing, which over a period of time had become his obsession. Many a times this obsession of his fuelled-up arguments between Dev and Neena. Dev, a history professor, had an aversion for business and everything associated with it- finance, taxes, investment...everything. And Neena's pressure on him to help her father in business had always remained a very sensitive issue between them. As far as Loveena's memory could unveil itself she remembered it as a dreaded subject, with her father's lost gaze accompanied by a stern silence, a clear indication of his repudiation flaring up her mother's temper.

The same subject was broached with different perspectives a number of times, sometimes by Neena and sometimes by her parents, albeit eliciting the same response from Dev. Neena's parents' advancing age and Dev's adamance to budge from his stance regarding the business and other property-related matters finally culminated with the winding off of all these things, except only this one property at

Orchard Street. After all, Neena had always desired to spend their life after Dev's retirement in the serenity of the hills.

When both of Loveena's parents were alive then also they had only occasionally visited the place. So, to ensure its security and maintenance, Neena's father had deputed one of his known and reliable persons- Ramchand to the outhouse of the property.

But after Dev's passing away, layers of grief and deteriorating health were enough to stifle the vestiges of Neena's materialistic inclinations. Over the past six years, since the time Dev had passed away, having little to no interest left in the place anymore, Neena made it a habit to phone Ramchand every once or twice a month and felt her duty discharged. She had also befriended the neighbours during her short stays over there who had promised her to brief about any issue if ever it arose, which rarely did.

Her assignment as an associate professor with the English department of the university was enough to keep Loveena occupied physically and mentally, in addition to providing financially, the latter never having been an issue with her. With this, she was also neither left with any time nor a desire to go to Banikhet.

But now, with the longing to get a respite from her choppy life, she had decided to leave her old life behind into solitude in a place away from the chaos of the city, away from the sympathetic eyes of her neighbours, colleagues and known ones. Moreover, a surge of a feeling of guilt for neglecting the house, which was so close to her mother's heart, arose within her aching heart.

But is it really what the world is? Is the ever-changing state of mind with the ever-changing state of worldly relations the only theme behind this magnificent creation? Is experiencing this illusion of relations and emotions the only thing into which this grand journey of life be summed up? Or is life about experiencing something more profound, permanent and blissful lying hidden somewhere beneath the shallowness of all these illusions, which forms the core of the existence of everything? But to find it, to experience it one has to dive into the depths obscured by the shallowness of these illusions.

HELP FROM A STRANGER

"The world is a *menacing place*. Don't trust anybody."

She felt her mother's voice whisper in her ear.

"I know." She muttered under her breath.

Standing on the platform in a state of limbo for some time, a board with a *Help Desk Counter* inscribed on it in bold letters hanging on the wall near the exit of the platform caught her attention. An arrow was pointing in the direction of the counter. Her brain was in a state of indecisiveness and devoid of any itinerary, and Loveena having no dearth of time, was in dire need of some external assistance to decide her future course of action. *Help* was the only thing she needed at that time to settle the jargon of her thoughts. Pulling her luggage, she started moving in the direction of that arrow. After dragging herself for a few hundred meters she arrived at the help desk counter. A small group of foreign tourists were already present there.

"Huh...how could one gather so much energy to cross the wide expanse of oceans, mountains, deserts...only to reach an unknown place with indecipherable language and an alien culture?"

Loveena's big, brown eyes widened with curiosity fixated on that group, as if to see through them to find their hidden source of energy. A bubbly troop of youngsters dressed in bright clothes was lending vibrance to that otherwise bland corner of the platform. Irrespective of their gender, everyone had long hair which were kept in place by tying them into ponytails or with headbands. Enthusiasm was exuding from their chirpiness. *Every human emotion is enigmatic, powerful enough to influence everyone it comes in contact with.* The enthusiasm of those tourists also lent a heightened spirit not only to the environment but also to the weary soul standing behind them.

While waiting for her turn, Loveena felt herself getting immersed in the euphoria of their enthusiasm and felt the tightness of the nerves in her brain loosen up, giving her relief. She was in no hurry. Neither did she have anybody waiting for her nor did she have any love for the place she was going to. So, what to hurry for?

And she developed an instant interest in the situation.

The fat and pudgy man, in charge of the counter, with his limited knowledge of English, and the foreigners with their limited access to very few Hindi words were all struggling hard to make each other understand themselves. For a moment she thought of mediating their conversation, but then her brain, already overburdened with working out the possibilities, probabilities and likely outcomes of the decision which she was going to take, muted all the outside sounds making her immune to the discussion taking place at the counter. Her eyes settled on that pudgy man, analysing him to understand whether he could be trusted or not. This was the only lesson her mother had always made her practice again and again.

"Don't trust anybody," her mother whispered to her head again.

When her brain got tired of all that inconclusive analysis, it again hibernated. Now she was merely watching the man at the counter without seeing him. His bright maroon satin shirt was going well with his fair complexion, but its buttons appeared to be struggling hard to keep the front halves of his shirt together. And the bulge of stomach hidden beneath his white vest was trying hard to release itself from the clutches of the satin shirt. This struggle was akin to the struggle of words between him and the foreigners at that time. He gouged out a big bite from a deep-fried samosa lying on a plate on his counter, tattling the reason for his pudginess.

　　　　　HELP FROM A STRANGER

Every bite accompanied by a sip of tea, slowly making its way to some corner of that bulge, was seemingly putting more pressure on those poor buttons.

This thought elicited a mischievous smile on Loveena's face.

Subconsciously she was counting the seconds with the same eagerness that she had once done on the day her high school English teacher Ms Shabana had fallen off the stool she was sitting on. Ms Shabana was one of the few teachers for whom not only Loveena but most students in the class had no liking for.

Ms Shabana… the contours of her oval face and the cloistered meanness of her small eyes accentuated by her tightly tied hair into a top knot bun. The big mole on her chin appeared to be God's afterthought addition to complete that look. Her small eyes which narrowed down with the ferocity of her temper made everybody dread with terror. She drew pleasure in punishing her students. One day a few boys in her class, to settle some score with her, replaced her caned chair with one having a cracked leg that could give away any moment after she sat on it.

In the class of forty students, with each one sitting on individual benches arranged in four rows, Loveena was the one sitting in the front row. Eagerness to see her teacher crashing on the ground was akin to that of watching the fate of that fated button.

Thawak, the cracking sound of the wooden leg of the stool superimposed that of breaking of the button and falling of the button somewhere on the ground…. just like Ms Shabana.

The bulge successfully attaining freedom, covered beneath the white of the vest, in stark contrast to the shiny marron of the satin shirt left the pudgy man flustered.

"Mission accomplished."

Loveena felt a strong urge to break into laughter *when her mother scolded her.*

"What childish behaviour Loveena. You are a grown-up girl. Behave gracefully."

"Madam, how may I help you?" The exhaustion and embarrassment from the incidents of the past hour were spilling from his voice. He was nervously pulling down his short black tie to cover the white of his vest.

With this Loveena came out of her trance, cursing herself for the absurdity of her thoughts that made her forget the purpose for which she was standing there in front of that counter.

"Hmm…I have to go to Banikhet. But now that it is getting dark, I am thinking of spending the night here. So could you please help me book a room in some good hotel?"

This seemed to be a question he had faced with most of the inquirers, making him feel comfortable and regaining some of his confidence, which was visible in the way he started giving her options and possibilities. While talking to her, he kept dialling numbers on the telephone lying in front of him, pausing his talks with her and talking to the person on the other side of the line. Maybe he was talking to the people at the receptions of different hotels. With not an iota of knowledge about the hotels and the place she felt a dread arise within her.

"Don't let him know that you are alone and new to the place. Otherwise, he could take advantage of your situation." Mother whispered again.

Unaware of the struggle going on inside her brain, the pudgy man was busy calling different hotels. With the good hotels reeling under the burden of overbooking, he advised her against staying in the lesser-known hotels in not-so-good localities. And out of

       HELP FROM A STRANGER

sympathy arising from the situation she was in, he suggested her to spend the night in the waiting lounge of the railway station.

"Are you going by taxi or by bus in the morning?"

Hearing this, she perspired in the month of October. *"Oh! How could anybody be so stupid like you? You have still not attained the maturity to make sensible decisions..."* Her mother's blabbering was further agitating her perplexed mind.

"I haven't thought about it yet," replied Loveena in a meek voice. "Suggest to me what would be the most comfortable for me."

Saying this, she shifted the onus of her arrangements to the hands of a person stranger to her to the extent of her being unfamiliar with even his name.

"Oh, my poor child! What are you doing? Trusting a stranger! Where have all my teachings gone?" Loveena felt her mother lambasting her stupidity.

"What will happen in Banikhet?"

The popping up of her mother's questions in her mind kept adding to her inner disquiets.

Unaware of the doubts arising in Loveena's mind, the pudgy man was busy making phone calls to book a taxi for her further journey. The helpful nature of the person suddenly pushed the pendulum of her thoughts towards the trait she was born with - to have faith in and to trust people. And a faint smile appeared on her lips.

"Thank you."

JOURNEY

*I*rrespective of the enormity of decades lived through, only a few lines are needed to summarize the whole life. A few lines...a few moments...a few incidents...and the whole of life spent is summed up. Is it magical or ironic? When with every breath, life is equally distributed in every moment of the day of the year of the life passed by then why only a few of them are retained or picked up by the mind, ignoring all others? Why do only a few moments leave their mark in memory making all others lost in oblivion? *The truth is that they had all passed without our living in them or feeling them .... or life is really a story of a few moments narrated in decades.*

Loveena too was not an exception. With the matrix of her life strongly woven around only very few relations, every memorable moment of her life shone brightly like a crystal in that matrix. And she always imagined those crystals shining brightly in the hues of red, white and yellow- the colours she loved. Thus, she assigned them to the relations she possessed.

"Babli," shrieked Neena.

Loveena, about three years of age sitting on the floor with her face hidden beneath the red, brown and mauve of her mother's lipsticks, lying scattered around her with babysitter Babli standing near her. Babli laughed and so did Loveena.

... Babli - the source of all her childhood memories.

Loveena ran from one room to another, and Babli followed her.

Loveena ate her food, and Babli waited upon her and cleaned her face.

Loveena scattered her toys, and Babli packed them.

Loveena cried, and Babli wiped up her tears.

And Loveena laughed...Babli laughed.

But now, Neena's shriek made Babli tremble, silencing Loveena.

Often, we dig into our memories in search of the one that we can claim to be the first one to leave its mark on our lives. This certainly was that one memory for the little Loveena. It could also be assigned to be the first one in which her innocent mind had awarded her mother with the blue riband.

Be it her mother's praise or anger or worry...Loveena always felt her mother's presence all around her, all within her - thus making her attribute red to her mother. With that first shriek of Neena and its impact on Babli, Loveena's innocent mind accepted her mother as the boss of the family. And with years adding to her age, she found her mother's presence in all the aspects of their household...taking care of their family, looking after her grandfather's business...She was everywhere. So mother was to be obeyed, to be followed, to be believed...

But with her father Dev, Loveena always felt a sense of confusion arises within. *Parents are just to be loved and not to be analyzed.* But to love them and to weave them in the memories and stories some threads of theirs are required. Doing this is as difficult as painting on a sheet of water where different colours intermingle so effortlessly and perfectly forming an amazing hue that is difficult to even imagine. And so, Dev's calmness, which Neena claimed to be his indifference towards the family, pushed Loveena hard into looking for any positive aspect of this behaviour. And ultimately, she attributed this trait to his detachment...a trait considered not only respectable but saintly in humans.

...or maybe her mother's fierceness had made Dev retract into a shell...

But this forlorn thought about her mother always made her cringe and roused a feeling of guilt within, bringing her thoughts to an abrupt halt. She attributed detachment to be a trait of her father, making him an admirable person in her life and... memories.

The yapping of a dog nearby stifled her thoughts. Of late she had developed the habit of divulging deep into her thoughts, making herself immune to the surroundings. This enclosure... or cocoon, enclosing her with her thoughts, provided her with the comfort of not being alone anywhere. But the truth she failed to realize was that this habit of hers not only made her lonely even in a crowd but also never allowed her inner self to be at peace.

Hmm...but isn't it the first step towards self-realization...to listen to the inner self? And to listen, one needs to have patience. Ah...listening... patience...two most precious gems from the precious treasure of the soul that everybody is provided with but only a few endure.

She had been sitting in that waiting hall for the past two hours, but it was only now that she had noticed that there were three other families, two of whom were with little kids.

The taxi driver that the pudgy man at the help desk had arranged for Loveena was quite punctual and arrived very early in the morning when the darkness of the night sky had just started mellowing down with the stirring in of the white, giving a glimpse of the day hidden beneath. When the driver, an acquaintance of the pudgy man, came looking for her in the waiting lounge, she was sitting huddled on the bench. The slight chill and freshness of the emerging day seemed incapable of wiping out the lassitude from the previous day's journey and sleepless night which was revealing itself through her puffy and drowsy eyes. The anxiety of travelling in the mountainous region had also aggravated that weariness. The very thought of which was sufficient to make her nauseous as the memories from her earlier trips with her parents, which were very few and many years back, were also not much pleasant, with her throwing up on every turn and bend of the road, of which there were so many that she failed to keep a track of their count.

"Madam, I am Jagat Ram. Deepak Saab has sent me to take you to Banikhet."

"Deepak Saab! Who?"

"Deepak Saab from the help desk counter."

"Oh!"

It was only at that moment that she realized that she had not even thought that that man at the help desk could have a name other than the *pudgy man*. The absurdity of this perturbing thought engulfed all her weariness, making her wide awake.

Jagat Ram, a talkative and cheerful lad in his early twenties, exuberating joy and enthusiasm, didn't take much time to make Loveena feel comfortable. With the commencement of their journey began Jagat Ram's exposition of knowledge about the region, with him narrating to her the historical, cultural, and religious importance attached to almost every place or monument passing by, slowing down the vehicle so that Loveena could have a satisfactory view of it. So elaborate were his descriptions as if he was a witness to every happening of the past that had occurred many decades ago.

Loveena tried to show her interest by interjecting his monologue here and there with the monosyllables.

"So, you must be getting a lot of tourists here?"

"Not that many because the government has not adequately advertised all these things that I am telling you. So, the tourist potential of the place is yet to be exploited." He said with a sheepish grin.

"Drivers are just like that –always proud of their driving capabilities and knowledge about the terrain they are driving through. Always self-obsessed with their intelligence..." Dev's words reverberated in Loveena's ears.

"...even if they don't have it." An irritated Neena cut short Dev's sentence completing it herself.

"Papa you were right." Loveena sitting in the back seat of the car muttered to herself in response to a statement made by her father so many years ago to pacify her mother of the anger that was boiling inside her for an act of their driver, Surjeet Singh. And what he did flashed before her eyes.

Surjeet Singh was their family driver her grandfather had sent down from the town of Bardha to serve his daughter Neena in the city. Their big and sprawling house nestled amidst lush greenery was on the outskirts, close to the university where Dev taught but far off from the city. So, within a short span of time, Surjeet ferrying Neena to and fro from the market or to a friend's house in the city became an indispensable part of her life.

It was on one such visit to her friend's place that the incident happened which left Neena boiling in rage over Surjeet. But later on, that very incident had acquired the status of an amusing anecdote which Neena loved to describe to every acquaintance of theirs and never without extracting a guffaw of laughter. And this was the only incident that Surjeet must have wanted to erase from Neena's memory.

It happened on a fine day when Neena decided to pay a visit to her friend in the city who had given birth to a baby. On the pretext of buying some rolls and muffins for the friend's elder daughter Neena stopped at the baker's shop in the market. While she was waiting for her turn to make payments, the sickly boy who worked at the baker's and was quite familiar with Neena, she being a frequent visitor, carried her bag to her car where Surjeet was waiting for her. The sickly boy, after putting the bag on the backseat closed the door with a bang. And when Neena returned after making the payment she found Surjeet missing. She searched...and searched... and searched...and then got baffled on not getting any clue of his whereabouts. Then under the scorching heat of the summer afternoon sun, she dragged herself to the nearest bus stop to catch a local bus to return to her house. When she arrived , she was red both with rage and the unbearable heat of the afternoon.

The mystery of Surjeet's disappearance was blasting her mind. But very soon it was solved.

On hearing the bang of the door, after the sickly boy at the baker's put that packet on the backseat, Surjeet without looking back ignited the engine and started towards their destination– Neena's friend's place. And it was only after reaching there that he looked back only to find Neena missing. With her missing and the packet lying there, he was gripped with panic.

"Where is *didi*...where is she?"

"Oh! She might have fallen somewhere in between."

With this thought, he was baffled and perspired with a wave of fear arising within him.

He turned his car around and rushed to the university to inform Dev about the tragedy. By the time he reached university and entered Dev's room, Neena was back at her house dialling Dev to tell him about missing Surjeet.

"Saab, *didi* has fallen somewhere." Surjit's words, frightened demeanour and tear-filled eyes were enough to panic Dev.

Tring, tring.... The harsh ringing of the telephone lying on the table at that moment further added to his anxiety. With trembling hands, Dev picked up the phone.

"Dev, Surjeet is missing." Neena's words from the other side of the line, though adding to Dev's confusion, acted as a pacifier for his racing heart.

That whole evening Surjeet kept sitting in the courtyard seeking Neena's forgiveness, and requesting her to not tell anybody about this incident.

The memory of this humorous incident lingered in their minds forever.

Changes are never drastic but always subtle- whether in nature or life. And the chill in the air and the appearance of the far-off hills were also the subtleties of that change.

"Madam, this checkpoint is the interstate boundary."

Stopping his car and parking it on one side of that not-so-broad road, Jagat Ram pulling out some documents from the glove compartment walked towards a wooden hut-like structure where two policemen were sitting outside checking some documents.

She had last visited the place about fifteen years ago along with her parents. That was also against her wish. Dev was also reluctant to come. So, it was only after a lot of cajoling from Neena that both agreed to accompany her. At that time, she was at the pinnacle of youth, accustomed to the pompous ways of city life. For Dev, his aversion to travelling made him reluctant to go there. But it was her grandfather's property in Banikhet, whose maintenance became her mother's responsibility after her grandparents passed away. With Dev not interested in taking over Neena's father's business or looking after their properties, everything became Neena's responsibility.

After the winding up of Neena's father's business, many of his properties were sold off. And the money received was stowed away in banks as fixed deposits. The property at Banikhet was the one closer to Neena's heart so she kept it. When Loveena's grandparents were alive, Neena used to visit the place with them. But after they were gone it became a challenge for her to cajole Dev and Loveena to accompany her to visit that house.

Loveena could now see the verdure of dense lush green vegetation and lofty trees having massive girths in the backdrop of far-off mountains which had been worked out by nature with consistent efforts of decades only to be overlooked by the overworked minds of most of the travellers, who were always in a rush to reach their destination. Sitting in the backseat of the car, with her gaze fixed on the outside scenery, these thoughts sprang up in her mind and she realized that she herself was also one of those travellers. Despite having visited that place a few times before, it was the first time that she was observing the surroundings so keenly. A gush of cool breeze touched her face ruffling her hair as if acknowledging her thoughts. The branches of trees swaying slowly under the impact of the cool breeze seemed refreshing and welcoming to Loveena's tired soul, uplifting her spirit.

"You might have been a witness to the bygone century and who knows how many centuries are still there waiting to get unfolded in your presence...You might also be the witness to my earlier trips with my parents," heaving a deep sigh she muttered to herself. With her intense gaze fixed on the dense forests on either side of the not-so-broad metalled road, she instantly felt a sense of camaraderie with them.

With a bang Jagat Ram, who had returned from the check post, closed the door of the car behind him, bringing her out of her thoughts.

With the increasing steepness of the mountainous road, the steepness of the bends makes Jagat Ram stretch over the steering wheel to control it. The narrowness of the road was to the extent that it was impossible for the vehicles coming from opposite directions to cross one another. With mountains on one side and a deep gorge on the other, it was certainly a test of Jagat Ram's driving skills. Many bends were lined with remembrance stones in memory of travellers whose vehicles had skidded down into the gorge at that place, making one realize the fragility of life. The tranquility of the environment and realization of the uncertainty of life dazed Loveena who was now sitting with her breath held up.

"Madam, that was the residence of some British officer in the colonial era, which, after independence was converted into a guest house." The silence was stirred up by Jagat Ram's voice breaking her chain of thoughts. He was pointing towards a magnificent old building on one side of that narrow road, visible from a distance. Its gabled roof painted in bright green camouflaged with the green of the surroundings making it indistinguishable from the distance. As they passed by, she noticed a black coloured iron plate, with *Dak bungalow* scribbled on it in bold letters, hanging between two poles, moving to and fro with the wind.

With Jagat Ram pointing out and showing her many more structures from the colonial era and with Loveena watching everything with interest and imagining the life of people who had lived there in some space of time in past, she was approaching her destination.

JOURNEY

ORCHARD STREET

*I*t's been long since the country gained freedom from British rule, but the fervour for British culture and language is so deeply ingrained in the psyche of people that over a period it has synonymized itself with the elite of the society. That might be the only reason that must have led the authorities or the residents to christen that small locality on the hilltop in Banikhet with the name *Orchard Street*. Neither were there any orchards nor was it a street. Contrary to the bustling and noisy streets of the town, the prevailing silence all around presented the solitariness of the street as well as of the life of families living there.

It was late in the evening when Loveena's taxi, after bearing the torture and trauma of climbing up the steep, spiral mountainous path had come to a rumbling halt in front of a house at the end of Orchard Street-her destination. There stood before her a beautiful cottage with *Lakshmi Niwas* scribbled in bold red letters in English and Hindi on the metalled brass plate fixed on the stone wall of the entrance. Her mother Neena, a religious and superstitious woman, like most Indian women, was in the habit of putting auspicious signs on every precious possession of hers, had put a big *Swastik* sign above *Lakshmi Niwas*. With this memory of her mother came rushing back the emptiness and hollowness which she dreaded and which she thought she had left behind closed in the house in the city. But now expecting the same hollowness, emptiness lying scattered in the cottage awaiting eagerly to receive her, to grab her, made her shudder in anticipation. The fatigue of the journey and her fears suddenly left her drained of her energy and desire to move, to open the door of the car and to come out.

"Madam."

She found the driver staring back at her with confusion.

"Any problem, madam?"

"Nah," she mumbled opening the door with one hand, clutching her purse in the other.

Jagat Ram also got out to open the trunk of the car, pulling her suitcase and handbag out of it. The noise created was sufficient to pierce the stiffness of the night of the mountains, alerting Ramchand and Manju, with both running out to receive her.

"Namaste babyji," welcomed Manju in a jubilant voice, with Ramchand following her with a warm smile on his face.

Loveena's earliest memory of Ramchand dates to the time when she was a small kid and Ramchand was a young lad who was recently married to Manju. Ramchand- lean, thin with medium height was filled with agility to sustain the life of hills. And Manju, an expert cook, equally lean, thin, energetic but much shorter than him. They both complemented each other, *an essentiality required for leading a successful married life.*

In all of Loveena's visits, whether accompanying her grandparents or parents, Ramchand and Manju were the static factors -always there to welcome them.

Time is invisible but the signs of its passing by get sprinkled everywhere. Ramchand, with his slightly stooping shoulders, the black of his hair replaced completely by the silver grey and deep wrinkles making their way to his forehead, jaws and wherever else they could find a place to settle in. And Manju, with the sheen of youth long lost, with her fair complexion hidden beneath the dark blemishes suddenly made Loveena realize the long time that had elapsed since she last met them -maybe a decade...or even more.

"Namaste. How are you?" Responded Loveena folding her hands.

But at that moment, in their presence, she felt her hollowness somewhat moderating, less haunting *and... bearable.*

THE FIRST ENCOUNTER

"Help...help...help..."

"*B*urrr...wow....burrr..." The calm and stillness of the sunny morning, slightly soaked in the chill of approaching winter, was drilled with the loud shrieks of a male followed by the incessant barking of a dog.

The whole mayhem was enough to wake Loveena up from her slumber. The previous day's long journey, the cold weather of the hills and nothing better to do in the whole day lying ahead of her were the deterrents to her leaving the snugness of bed.

The yelping of a man and barking of a dog was now interrupted by a kid's loud shouts of *Sherry, Sherry* in a voice full of enthusiasm.

Throwing away her quilt, getting up from the bed, she pulled aside the heavy curtains from the floor-length glass windows. In an instant, the cold darkness of the room was suffused with the soft brightness and warmth of the morning sun. The hastiness in Ramchand and Manju's gait while crossing the distance to the main entrance of the cottage was visible to her. But the huge tree with its fully spread branches edging the bounding wall of the cottage near the entrance obstructed the view of the happenings on the road from Loveena's eyes.

By the time she came downstairs and reached the iron gate, Ramchand and Manju were already standing there. The intensity of fear was being expressed clearly in their wide-open eyes and bated breaths at that moment. Fear had numbed their senses to the extent that they failed to notice the appearance of Loveena on the scene. And Loveena...in no time after throwing a glance at the elderly couple also inadvertently joined them in their expressions- wide open eyes with bated breath.

On the narrow road in front of their house was standing a portly, dark-complexioned man with a yellow *chandan* mark on his forehead. He was the victim. Despite the chill in the weather, he was perspiring profusely with beads of sweat shining under the rays of morning sun falling on his face. Freshly applied *chandan* on his forehead had started running down along with the sweat droplets in the form of fine stream smearing the bridge of his nose. He was wearing a white shirt and a white *dhoti*. His *dhoti* which earlier must have been wrapped around his protruding belly was now in a tattered condition with its one end tightly flinched between the sharp teeth of a bulky dog and the other end tightly secured by that man in an effort to save his modesty. With neither of the parties in the mood to let go of their end, it seemed to be a tug-of-war between them. A chubby-cheeked turbaned kid, around ten years of age, standing close to the dog, shouting *Sherry, Sherry* like a cheerleader, was sending the dog into a frenzy aggravating the situation.

A smaller and equally chubby girl, probably the boy's sibling, was standing near him, laughing and enjoying herself.

All this bucked up that burly dog making him gritty and gnash his teeth, besides sending shivers down the spines of all the spectators. The whole drama was accelerating the production of the sweat glands of the trembling victim in that chilled environment.

A faint giggle from across the wall of Loveena's house attracted everybody's attention. A malnourished sickly man was laughing into his hands. In that moment that giggle was enough to make him the focus of the happenings, embarrassing him. And to escape from it, he ran inside. "He is Palaram, our neighbour Mr Shastri's servant. His behaviour is always bizarre," whispered Manju.

"H.. h... helppp..." stammered the victim collecting the last remnants of courage left behind in him, bringing the situation back on track.

Just then Loveena saw a short and heavily built lady, dressed in a bright green *salwar kameez*, running out from a house, two houses down the lane. She was running towards the dog. Her fair round face was getting red with anger. Her annoyance was oozing not only from her face but also from her shouts of *Sherry...Harry... Simmi*. It was only then that the stubborn dog opened his mouth making that man free and sending him into hysteria hurling curses and abuses towards the dog, those two children and their parents.

When the scene appeared to be settling down, an unexpected occurrence provided a little more life to the dying incident. It was the emergence of a turbaned man from the same house as the lady. He walked leisurely towards them calling *Simran, Simran*. He was the father of those children.

"*Satsriakal* Reddyji," the turbaned man jovially greeted the victim, who was still trembling under the aftermath of the tragedy, overlooking or maybe ignoring the gravity of the situation.

"I have told you so many times that our Sherry can never hurt anybody and moreover he is properly vaccinated."

It's not the first time that such an incident has happened here. The turbaned man's words implicitly made it clear to Loveena.

"And I suggest you to wear *pyjamas* instead of a *dhoti* as I think Sherry doesn't like *dhoti* or maybe they seem playful to him. Ah..." putting stress on the last monosyllable accompanied by sideways movement of head so as to express his utter distress and hopelessness, the turbaned man continued "Reddyji why don't you understand that Sherry is an animal, but you are a human being and more intelligent than him. So please understand...And I promise if Sherry does the same thing with *pyjamas,* then we will sit together and discuss what to do further..." The turbaned man was speaking in fluent Punjabi. This long sermon left everybody surprised and with this, the turbaned man had captured all their attention which was earlier focused on Sherry.

Moreover, Loveena was sure that not a word of it would have made any sense to the victim.

"Ah...it's good that that fellow is not understanding anything otherwise the situation could have become more explosive," thought Loveena. The blank look on Reddyji's face and the emptiness in his eyes with which he was staring at the turbaned man was a clear indication of that.

Reddyji, the poor victim, who was listening but not understanding even an iota of the sermon with his flaring nostrils, now unable to control his anger, started shouting in a language nobody understood, probably his mother tongue. But this made Reddyji's wife come out running from the house adjacent to that of the turbaned man. She came, and without saying anything to anyone collected the torn-out *dhoti* in one hand, pulled her husband with the other, and took him inside.

The speed with which the whole incident unfolded, displaying a plethora of emotions left Loveena, Ramchand and Manju speechless. With Reddy ji now gone inside, leaving behind a group of amused spectators, the turbaned man looked towards Loveena greeting her with *satsriakal.*

Loveena, who was feeling a surge of guilt arise within her on not getting angered but amused by the incident, greeted him back. Now the dog, the kids, the woman and the man - all of them squeezed around Loveena's gate forming a small group.

The man introduced himself, "Myself Harsimran, my wife Harsimran aka Simran, my son Harsimran aka Harry, my daughter Harsimran aka Simmy and our dog Sherry."

This introduction made Loveena's eyes pop out with curiosity or shock or confusion or.... or she herself was unable to understand. But she partially understood the very first lesson on the very first morning of her arrival in Orchard Street that *life is not as serious a matter as had always been projected.*

 THE FIRST ENCOUNTER

INSIGHT

Whether people change places to break their monotonous lives or places change people to get respite from their eternal monotonicity- is a debatable question. But whatever the inference, one certain thing is – the desire for change. And this change had worked wonders with Loveena's restless soul. It started experiencing calmness as a result of fuzzing out of its disturbing thoughts, bringing occasional smiles to her face. With the opulence of time at her disposal, the hastiness of city life started to settle down, making her realize a serene calmness in every passing moment, kindling in her a desire to explore the place which she visited earlier also but without feeling any inclination or urge to get connected to. Orchard Street was the same but with a transforming outlook about life, her senses were perceiving every sensation of the surroundings with the likeness of a sponge, absorbing everything minutely and then rubbing it on her broken heart, ultimately squeezing out everything into her soul, every time cleansing bits of darkness covering it.

The brick-lined small terrace of the cottage had caught hold of a tender spot in her heart. The silence of the surroundings reverberated with her inner silence. She was amazed by the ability of nature to keep its silence intact despite the clamour of worldly affairs taking place in it, contrary to which even a single incident is enough to storm the inner calm, inner silence of the human mind. Standing against the wrought iron railing of the terrace, the vast expanse of the dense forests and the gorges and streams bared themselves before her. It is only when nature begins to bare itself that the journey of life, the journey of the soul –the spiritual journey begins in a real sense.

The dense forest having a diversity of pines, deodars, oaks, rhododendrons and wild grasses and shrubs covering every inch of the naked land gave it a velvety appearance from a distance. Amidst all the greens was visible a streak of white which Ramchand told her was a wide stream of water originating somewhere in the mountains. The distance was the culprit for reducing its vastness to a fine streak. The shades of green of the leaves and grasses and varied hues of wildflowers in the backdrop of the spotless white snow-covered mountains under the reflection of the sun's rays resembled some broad canvas. Sitting transfixed for hours with an intent gaze fixed on those snow-capped mountains she was amazed by the adaptability of the white colour. She observed keenly how the whiteness of snow gets transformed into gold with the magical touch of yellow of the sun's rays falling on it only to subsequently and silently transform itself into a sparkling silver on moonlit nights. The ease with which the white of magnificent peaks shone with the brilliance of gold and silver, was equivalent to the ease with which that sparkling white got itself obscured beneath the blanket of darkness of moonless nights.

Was it the adaptability of the white colour or the humility of those mountains, which kept adapting themselves silently and gracefully to the changing circumstances? Unlike humans....

The yard of the cottage with its velvety grass and a rainbow of colours scattered in a variety of azaleas, petunias, marigolds, and roses with all the intricacies of Ramchand's gardening expertise was in tandem with the surroundings.

Sitting in a cane chair on the terrace, soaking herself in the warmth and brightness of the morning sun had become one of the few things that Loveena relished. She used to sit there to enjoy the beauty of nature scattered all around her. But with the passing days, weeks, and months her sight which earlier was just seeing nature, was now with the calming down of her inner restlessness becomes more observant and responsive to even the minutest of changes taking place in her surroundings. She had started noticing the growth pattern of the potted money plants, with them taking an upward growth without getting deterred by the adversity imposed by their flaccid stem. She noticed the opening of the tiny buds exposing their inner beauty in the form of beautiful flowers. She observed that the corner of the terrace, which never got sufficient sunlight to dry up the dampness accumulated by the misty nights, had transformed itself into a breeding ground for algae, supporting a small patch of green and orange on it. Everything in nature was changing, everything was growing up and celebrating that change and growth by exuding its hidden beauty.

Then what had made her own growth so devastating, so painful? Then what had happened to her growth that instead of making herself familiar with the beauty of the soul she was born with, it got obscured under the darkness of restlessness and despondency? Why wasn't her growth following the trajectory of nature? Either she was not a part of nature, or she failed to notice that change.

Sitting amidst that deep silence and tranquility of hills made her ponder over the thoughts which she never knew had existed in her mind.

Winters in the hills are spellbinding. The penetrating chill of the evening air seems like natures's attempt to stir the dormant soul which one forgets is lying asleep somewhere deep within. The mist and fog of the evenings resembling a thin veil makes one realize the existence of a veil within engulfing the soul, preventing one from communicating with it and listening to its faint voice. And the stillness of the surroundings with its huge pine and deodar trees, with its snow-capped majestic mountains, with the penetrating chill hovering silently all around ...everything appears to be listening attentively to the whispers of the universe which a human mind with all its internal chaos fails to listen. But when a disciple becomes eager to listen to nature, to pierce through the veil engulfing the soul, nature also starts attracting him so as to reveal the only lesson that the soul is yearning to listen to, to quench its thirst to merge itself with it, to feel that oneness -that which is eternal and can never be expressed in words.

"Babyji, it's getting cold here."

Manju's words brought Loveena out of her thoughts.

"It seems like ages had passed with me standing in this yard," said Loveena with a faint smile on her lips.

"It is the blessing that is bestowed down in the form of mist from those snow-capped mountains, the abode of Gods, the abode of Lord Shiva. It is the tranquility in it that one loses track of time, healing one's body and soul with its magical touch." Ramchand's feeble voice made both look in his direction.

He was approaching them after locking the iron gate at the entrance- his daily routine to prevent the entry of trespassers, which hardly were any. His flagging gait gave a glimpse of the years spent by him in these mountains.

"If you want to sit here, shall I put a bonfire?"

Hmm...she uttered, wrapping her shawl tightly around her shoulders.

The three of them sitting around the bonfire, in the darkness of moonless night, with their faces glowing softly in the warmth of the yellow flames were oozing out a strange calmness.

          INSIGHT

"Ramchand, what are your sons doing?"

"Living with their families in a nearby town."

Loveena remembered Ramchand as a doting father for whom the only joy was talking endlessly about his boys, which was quite contrary to his present conduct of summing up their lives in a single sentence. She sensed a feeling of indifference or... detachment in his voice which was still lingering in the silence that stretched out between the three of them. It was only after a few minutes that Manju broke that silence by telling her how their two sons had fought over their share in the piece of land that Ramchand handed over to them. And how both of themselves, Ramchand and Manju, merely acted as spectators with their sons bitching about each other. With both of their sons unwilling to listen to either of them, they decided to keep out of their ways.

"Don't you feel any anguish?"

"Hhh...Nah. Poor souls...they are trying to quench their thirst by accumulating as much as they can. Hmm...Everybody does. In the hope of getting happiness. But what they fail to realize is that by doing so they are merely trying to satiate their senses. But happiness...it is the thirst of the soul, lying deep within, beyond the reach of senses... uncorrupted by worldly illusions." Ramchand's voice, despite being weak, had the strength and clarity of wisdom which Loveena had never imagined to be so clearly ingrained in his thoughts.

"Everything that is expressed on the face of the earth, with the grace of Lord Shiva, vibrates with serenity and calmness. Listen to Mother Nature or the cry of a newborn...both are bestowed upon with purity. Because that's the only thing that He possesses- *purity.* Nature with its limited senses retained that purity but with human beings, the more their senses start perceiving, the more corrupted the purity of the soul gets. With this they start churning out negativities, engulfing their soul, thus creating chaos within and not without spreading out like smoke in the surroundings, creating jealousy, hatred, and animosity. But...then this is what we call *samsara*. My sons are also completely immersed in this *samsara*. So why feel anguish towards the people who are living in an illusion."

Manju was staring towards the snow-capped mountains with empty eyes without blinking, her folded hands lying motionless in her lap.

Loveena's eyes widened in acknowledgement on experiencing an insight into depths of worldly illusions, that she had never given a thought to. Besides acknowledgement were the shades of surprise-surprise which sprang out on hearing words of profound wisdom *from Ramchand.*

"Who is your *Master,* Ramchand?"

"*Master?*" Ramchand's repetition in his confused voice was enough to exhibit his ignorance of the word.

"*Master*...your *guru* from whom you have learned these ways of life."

"*Guru...* Mountains...with their treasure trove of virtues regarding calmness, stability, patience...have so much to learn from." Ramchand's feeble voice overflowing with reverence for the majestic mountains made Loveena contemplate his words.

So true...seasons, lacking stability, keep on changing...air lacking patience becomes furious, ocean lacking calmness displays its restlessness in its high rising tides...only mountains ...they are really the blessed ones to retain all the virtues irrespective of the everchanging circumstances...

"Babyji, if you can still your senses then only you can hear music, very fine music in the air. It is said to be originating from those snow-clad tips, the abode of Lord Shiva." His voice was feeble but unflinching and unwavering, overflowing with calmness, surrender and acceptance. His wrinkled face was illuminated with an aura making him appear like a mystic who had tasted the sweetness of the overflowing nectar of wisdom from the treasure of nature and had quenched the thirst of his soul, the ultimate desire of every being. Loveena, with her every breath, tried to take in as much as possible, healing herself and becoming more responsive, more childlike.

A moment like this is sufficient to set in motion the heart's yearning for many more moments like this and only then does it starts to tread that joyous journey of life which everyone is born to experience.

AURORA

When life is confined to nothing else but materialism, the heart also delves into the pleasures emanating from worldly achievements. And then it anxiously keeps count of every passing day. Each passing day makes it jittery over the ever-dwindling days of the life left behind. But in the absence of any materialistic desires, days just keep piling into weeks, weeks into months, finally giving way to years, without even getting noticed.

Time was passing at its own pace. But whether it was Loveena's sitting on the terrace soaking in the warmth and brightness of morning sun penetrating the unfathomable depths within or her strolling in the yard inhaling deeply the freshness of air overladen with the fragrance of flowers... to her, time had lost its relevance.

Orchard Street- a cluster of around twenty houses, distributed sparsely but with all having their entrance opening on the narrow, metalled road with an impediment on the other side beyond which lie a deep gorge. In the row of these houses, *Lakshmi Niwas* was the last one- situated on the dead end beyond which lay a small hill covered with dense vegetation. Loveena, with the strong impressions of her upbringing engraved in her mind, had always felt safe from all the perils of the outside world within the four walls of her house, and had thus confined herself within them. The sprucing up of her inner clutter of the long-acquired worldly traits initiated the blooming up of her dormant sensitivity to perceive the ethereal beauty of the world. Then she started experiencing a longing to explore her surroundings, making her emerge from the cocoon of tightly demarcated world of her house. The day she opened the main gate at the entrance of her cottage, coming out on that narrow-metalled road, walking downhill counting the number of houses of which she had counted twenty...yes twenty was the exact number that she confirmed. The twentieth house from *Lakshmi Niwas* was at the end of Orchard Street. At a distance of a few hundred meters from the last house was a small shop. And at a short distance from the shop, downhill, was a trail leading into the forest, which, after taking an upward bend led to the stream that was visible as a fine streak from the terrace of Loveena's cottage.

This small shop with *Sharma and Sons* scribbled in bold orange on the whiteboard fixed above the shutter at its entrance was in itself as magical as the box of a magician. Whether one demands a pair of socks or potatoes or a bottle of shampoo or even a glass of hot steaming tea...the thin boy with sunken tribal features, working as a helper in that shop, would appear with the item as if him saying *abracadabra* was how he could find everything in that shop. Besides providing the items, it also provided residents with the services of stuffing pillows, and quilts. So, in a word, the shop was...indispensable.

Being the only shop catering to all the essentials of daily life, it was frequented by the residents, developing acquaintances among them. And now Loveena had also joined that bandwagon, becoming a part of it.

Moreover, the owner, whom everybody addressed as Sharmaji, was a friendly man with a welcoming smile who always attended his customers with warmth. Besides all the services that this shop provided the residents with, it was the hotbed of gossip about the politics and happenings of that small town.

It was at this place that Loveena got acquainted not only with the residents but also with tidbits and upheavals of their lives through Sharmaji.

Loveena had come across the Reddys and the Harsimrans on her first day of arriving at Orchard Street. But it was only with the Harsimrans that her relations blossomed, maybe due to their free-spirited nature contrary to which Mr Reddy's reserved nature had projected the Reddys as uncommunicative. It was their reserved *or* cautious *or* complacent nature *or* disinterest in the social life *or* a clash of their culture *or* incompatibility with their immediate neighbours-the Harsimrans, or some other reason.... but they kept themselves wrapped up securely in a cocoon, dissembling their existence for the Orchard Street.

After spending many decades of her life in an overcrowded city, where even a little carelessness could lead to bumping into somebody on the street, where she had had so many students and colleagues in the university, where she was surrounded by so many neighbours and other people all the time, it was only now, in the confines of this small secluded locality amidst towering trees and mountains, that Loveena realized how limited *or more correctly negligible* her interactions with people had earlier been. She was living in the world but without feeling its ways, its texture. Now she had started to not only feel that texture but becoming a part of it...and she had started smiling, laughing and enjoying her existence... a new beginning for her.

BUDDING CAMARADERIE

Ramchand's outhouse in a corner near the main entrance of Loveena's cottage, frequented by the helpers of the adjoining houses, was always a hub of activity. But of all his visitors, Palaram was the regular one. Whenever he got a chance to escape from his employer Mr Shastri, he would barge into Loveena's house looking for Ramchand. While he always boasted of himself as a multitasker and posed to be overburdened with work at the Sashtris', he contrarily appeared to be free most of the time either standing near Ramchand tending the plants or sitting on the impediment on the road outside their house soaking in the warmth of the sun. Any call from Mrs Shastri usually fell flat on his ears but one from Mr Shastri drew his immediate attention. And Mr Shastri's appearance was what he dreaded the most.

The Shastri couple, Loveena's immediate neighbours, were considered to be one of the oldest ones in the locality and also the only ones who were the original inhabitants of the region, as was told by Mr Shastri himself to Loveena. With the life of the old couple confined not only by the boundaries laid down by surrounding hills but also by the years lying ahead, words had also lost their newness, making their narrations repetitive. So Loveena, while sitting on their lawn having a cup of tea, was also made to go through their...or more aptly his narrations with Mrs Shastri failing her guts to interrupt her husband.

Mrs Shastri, a short statured frail and bony woman having wheatish complexion, was the owner of a subdued personality. The way she meekly nodded at every statement of her husband gave a glimpse of her neglected stature in the household. Mr Shastri, also short-statured but sturdy and fair-complexioned, had a complicated personality with rapid mood swings. Even a single brief moment of his wife's interruption used to be enough to unplug the volcano of his anger. In that brief moment, the ease and pleasure of Mr Shastri's narrations would swiftly evaporate in the heat of his anger dripping from his suddenly reddened face and eyes, making the poor lady tremble under the impact of an intense furious gaze fixated on her. Sometimes a mere *intense* gaze from his wife was enough for her to be reprimanded by him, while sometimes he would lambast her with his harsh words, doing which seemingly soothed and satisfied his inner self. Witnessing such moments left Loveena in an uncomfortable situation. But at the same time, she also felt amazed at Mr Shastri's ability to transform, because the moment he turned his face towards Loveena he used to return to his former self- continuing with his narration from where he had left. But the agony of being meted out with that treatment which Mrs Shastri must have endured all through her married life had now settled comfortably and permanently in the wrinkles of the old lady's cheeks. Nevertheless, every fresh outbreak of Mr Shastri's temper would still pump her wearied face with embarrassment-reddening it with pain and shame. It was this fear of Mr Shastri that she never dared to speak anything except for nodding her head from time to time giving the impression of having some spring fixed in her neck that would start bobbing by even the slightest force of words emanating from her husband's mouth. The only times when Loveena had heard Mrs Shastri's feeble voice was to call Palaram.

Mr Shastri's commentaries from the past were the things that every inhabitant of the locality had listened to for the umpteenth time. Sometimes it was from the times of his great-grandfather about how they had served under the British Raj and the incidents and tidbits from that era narrating how the British were attracted to the region around Banikhet, resulting in them establishing settlements. Sometimes they were from the times of his childhood or youth that he had spent in the region studying in the local school, going to college in the neighbouring town or regarding his experiences as a Sanskrit teacher in a government school, and sometimes about his wanderings in the forests. While, per expectations, he never talked about his wife, who always kept sitting there supporting his every remark intermittently either with monosyllables or by the nodding of her head, never opposing him in anything. He, surprisingly very rarely talked about his only son.

His narrations progressed from fondness for the past to despondency of the present caused by his son leaving his native land to settle abroad and culminated in his apprehension of them being the last of their lineage living in Banikhet. While this seemed to be the compulsive component of all his narrations, Palaram would jerk him back to the present.

As soon as Mr Shastri's eye would catch sight of Palaram, sitting in some corner of the lawn, passing his time fumbling with a spade or lazily pulling out a weed plant from a flower bed, all his emotions exhibiting fondness, or despondency would evaporate in the heat of his rage.

"You useless fellow. Again, passing your time."

"Nah sa'ab."

Palaram in his faded shirt and patched pants draped over his wrist-sized waist and a bony face with skin so taut that even God might have felt the need to stretch it to optimum to cover the underlying skeleton... used to disappear pulling out pipe lying scattered in some corner of the lawn on the pretext of watering the plants. Then would start the next set of narrations from Mr Shastri- now centered around Palaram.

"Ah! Palaram...His presence in our house in itself is a story that can force even an atheist to believe in the power of destiny..."

And begin Mr Shastri's memoirs on Palaram who had come to their place a few years ago with the recommendation of Mrs Shastri's brother. Whenever Mr Shastri got furious with Palaram, Mrs Shastri had to also bear the brunt of that anger- something that always happened.

So, Mr Shastri was an excellent narrator...And so were the Harsimrans...And also the widow with snow-white hair and knees jammed like the rusted hinges of the door...

While Mr Shastri's tales were about his simple life, beginning with his ancestors belonging to the region, with him being born and brought up there, having served there all his life and now leading a retired life at the very same place where he was born, the Harsimrans' was a hard luck story. His ancestors had lived in Lahore in undivided India only to migrate at the time of partition.

It was much before the partition of India into India and Pakistan in 1947 that Harsimran's great-grandfather, who was a businessman in Lahore got some inkling of the unfortunate events of the future.

Lahore, a prominently Muslim-dominated region of undivided India was a hotbed of politics. The restlessness of the masses to gain freedom from the clutches of the three centuries-old British rule simultaneously paralleled the clash of ideologies of political titans of Indian politics. This kept on continuously stirring the emotions of different communities -predominantly Hindus and Muslims.

All discussions in hushed-up tones and whispers in closed circles- whether in drawing rooms or amongst the customers in shops or among the people standing in small groups were laced with the diminishing probability of the peaceful coexistence of both these communities. It was a difficult time to make difficult decisions. Whether to believe in the materialization of these subdued fears somewhere in the future and wrap up one's flourishing business only to start afresh at some faraway and unknown place, or to wait for some miracle to happen which can dissolve this slowly growing wall of distrust and hatred among these two communities.

Harsimran's great-grandfather, a man who had faith in his instincts, belonged to the former category. Despite his ancestors not having even crossed the boundary of their locality in Lahore, he decided to migrate to this hill station along with a few of his relatives and friends. With the whole of the country an alien place to them, how this hill station far away from Lahore became his great-grandfather's destination... even Harsimran himself was not much sure about it except for an explanation that small places with very little competition are always good for establishing new businesses. But whatever the reason, his decision had proved to be the right one with their spices soon capturing the market of not only Banikhet but also of the neighbouring towns. When his great-grandfather had reached this small town with a truckload of his belongings and his family, he had rented a small house in the town but with the riches they acquired, they had bought a lot of property and now owned the beautiful house in Orchard Street which had become their permanent address.

Loveena, being a good listener, attentively listened to every detail of theirs sensing pride and achievement accompanying their narrations. She herself, after having led a tumultuous life, had her own narrations, her own stories regarding life. No denying the fact that she could easily step into Mr Shastri or Harsimran's shoes, detailing a historical discourse of her own. Stories regarding the grandeur of her maternal grandparents' house, her pampered childhood...and many more. But with time she had started gaining a profound wisdom that the lives of ancestors, however grand they might seem to others, have their own travails and heartaches, which every generation has to pass through, but are always overlooked by the successors while glorifying them in their singsong tales. She never had the urge to narrate, but only listened without interruption.

Except for that one time when she asked Harsimran about the mystery behind everyone in his family sharing the same name- *Harsimran.*

The grandeur of the drawing room exhibited in the numerous antiques, the shining upholstery of majestic sofas, the silken drapery covering the large window glasses and a cosmic painting of the Golden temple covering one whole wall -everything gave a momentous illusion of trembling under the impact of Harsimran's guffaw and Simran's giggling, bringing up a wave of embarrassment over Loveena, visible in the sudden flushing of her cheeks bringing small beads of perspiration over her brow.

"Please excuse us for our weird behavior," apologized Simran.

"Now we are accustomed to being asked about this question the very first thing when we introduce our family and were surprised when you didn't ask at that time," continued Simran.

"Ours is an arranged marriage," carried on a sobered-up Harsimran. "It was merely a coincidence that both of us shared a common name, and we took it as an indication from the almighty that we are made for each other...and now I think it to be true also. What do you think Simran?" Laughed Harsimran.

"And then we decided to name our children also *Harsimran*...It means *to remember God.* Isn't it a blessed name?"

"Hmm...True...*to remember God*...the ultimate, the origin and climax of everything."

Everybody can be a narrator but only a few are good listeners...
and Loveena was one of them. An excellent listener-not only
listening to the words but inhaling the subdued feelings hovering
around them only for them to trickle down into her heart, to her
soul churning out wisdom. Enhancement of wisdom sharpened
her senses and made her immerse in the texture of the world of
which she was herself a part but had earlier neither got a chance
nor felt the need to divulge into. The more she got immersed, the
more she understood it.

From all that she heard and all that she saw, Loveena had now
concluded that deeds of the ancestors resonate in the way the
society treats their future generations. The outspokenness of
Mr Shastri and Harsimran, glorifying their past, earned them
respect in that small locality of Orchard Street thus establishing
them as representatives of the locality.

Orchard Street had only two representatives...but that was only
till Khatun Begum entered the Reddy household.

With time, the only thing that Loveena had come to know about
the Reddys was that Mrs Reddy was a highly obsessed person.
And it was not one single thing that she was obsessed with. From
cleanliness to the daily religious rituals, from dietary habits to every
nitty-gritty of routine life, her obsession was rooted everywhere.
She could be synonymized with obsession to the extent that it
could be likened to a disorder.

And Mr Reddy...He also shared his wife's obsessions. These were
further overshadowed by his habits of cursing and sulking. He
must have cursed the person responsible for pulling him out of
his mother's womb...was one of the jokes that kept making rounds
among his known ones.

Mr Reddy was a scientist with a virology lab with regional research
centres all over India, one of which was in Banikhet. He had been
transferred here around twelve years back from Bangalore. India

being a huge country, its north and south are diametrically opposite exhibiting diversities not only in cultural, traditional and linguistic aspects but also climatically. Being a native of south India this was more than enough to make him unhappy on getting transferred from the comfort of a familiar region to a far-flung town, somewhere in the hills of the northern region of the country. He had channeled all his resources and energy into getting his transfer cancelled. His efforts initiated with him approaching the higher officials of the department, the politicians, to every person he thought the matter could even be remotely associated with. Fumes of desperation gathered to the extent that forced him to approach even the peons whose only task was to wait upon those officers and politicians and to carry their files. But all his efforts had fallen flat without yielding the desired result. When such a disgruntled and hapless person is forced to serve somewhere, what else could be expected from him except his constant cursing?He cursed everything -cursed the authorities for opening the office at such a place, cursed the moment in which the decision to open the office in such a far-flung place was taken and ultimately it was fate, that is every helpless person's last refuge, that was cursed.

Being in his profession meant satisfying the curiosities of mankind by researching the unknown. But always dissatisfied with himself, with everything around him...What an irony!

The slightest change in the surroundings of that teensy weensy Orchard Street was enough to stir the slumber that it was doused in most of the time. These were the moments which pumped liveliness into the lives of the residents. The hiring of Khatun Begum for household chores and that also by the Reddys was not something insignificant to escape their eyes. The news spread like wildfire, becoming the centre point of their discussions -amongst the Harsimrans, the Shastris, Sharmaji, the old widow with hair as white as snow and knees jammed like the rusted hinges of a door... and the residents of the outhouses of these households.

　　BUDDING CAMARADERIE

"How could Mrs Reddy allow that shaggy lady to enter her house?"

"Mr Reddy is now provided with one more reason to grumble."

...and so on.

But why had they hired her? A mystery.

THE GOSSIPMONGER

Reddys belonged to that community of society in which the caste system had been trickling deep down into the foundations over decades and decades, making Khatun's hiring indigestible to everyone. And with their well-known obsession with cleanliness and hygiene, it was nothing less than a surprise for the people living in their vicinity. It was seldom that their neighbours themselves had been admitted to their place without earning an expression of strong displeasure from Mrs Reddy.

It didn't take much time for the ripples caused by the incident to die down. Soon the residents came to know about the back injury that Mrs Reddy had sustained after falling hard on the floor after getting unconscious, thus disabling her from moving. This was the reason that had sent Mr Reddy into a frenzy searching for domestic help. A lady for domestic help is a rare commodity in Orchard Street despite it being occupied predominantly by well-to-do families. It was with great efforts of his office staff that Khatun Begum had been revived out of her hibernation as a help. But Khatun was a character that could neither be ignored nor be tolerated, neither by Reddys nor by the other residents of the place.

Khatun Begum, a name overflowing with royalty, sophistication and graceful mannerisms, everything in sheer disagreement with the attributes of characters possessed by the owner of the name -a medium-built, dark-complexioned, middle-aged woman in tattered clothes- resembling a vagabond. Her dirty yellowish-white hair was covered under a discoloured and frayed *dupatta* and clapped-out slippers exposed her cracked heels...not one thing about her was compatible with the name she possessed- a combination of two honorifics to name a human being in pathetic and tattered condition. This was nothing more than a satire and Khatun Begum exemplified that.

Through her excellently fabricated stories, the Reddy couple whose life, with all their introversion had been cocooned inside the four walls of their house, now started to pandiculate itself before the gossip-starving society.

To be gossiped about, however disliked...probably is also an essential component of being weaved into the texture of the community, to become a part of it. Until Khatun Begum had entered the Reddy household, there was not much that people knew about them and without knowing much there was nothing much to be talked about. And when there is nothing to be talked about, then there is nothing to make one a part of that society. Khatun Begum was to be accredited for making the Reddys a part of the society *in which they already existed for the last many years.*

In addition to the gossips she brought out, Khatun Begum's frequent appearances aroused Loveena's interest in her. While sitting on her terrace or during her evening walks, she noticed Khatun Begum either entering or leaving Mr Reddy's house and every encounter was a divulgence into the efforts Mrs Reddy was putting in to make Khatun Begum look more presentable. It was reflected not only in her personal upkeep but also in the change of her garb. In a short span of time, Khatun had also become a character in the rambling stories of Orchard Street.

With Ramchand and Manju getting old, Loveena also hired Khatun Begum to provide her with cleaning services. Not only Loveena, but other residents of the locality had also started taking her services. The widow with snow-white hair hired Khatun to massage her jammed knees and Khatun who must not have ever massaged oil into her hair was massaging the knees of the widow. In a nutshell, Khatun Begum, contrary to her initial appearance, was quite a shrewd person who knew the ways of life.

Having no relation close enough to bear the inconvenience of coming up to Orchard Street to meet Loveena, the ringing of her doorbell was a rarity for her. It was one of those rare moments when, on a cloudy day, the sonorous sound of the bell struck Loveena's ears. Contrary to the other days when this sonorous sound of the bell would have rejuvenated her, breaking her monotony, today in the coldness of the cloudy day, she dragged herself out of her quilt. Standing on her terrace she found a young boy standing at the gate.

"*Mataji* has sent me to enquire about Khatun Begum. Did she come for work at your place today?"

Mataji was the name assigned as a mark of respect to the widow with snow-white hair by the residents of Orchard Street. She had, after a few months of services from Khatun, got accustomed not to her massage but to her company that provided her with a respite from her loneliness. It was from Khatun that Loveena had come to know about the differences between *Mataji* and her daughter-in-law, both of whom were living separately in different sections of the same house. Having lost her husband at a very young age *Mataji* had brought up her children- a daughter and a son- single-handedly. With her daughter now married to a schoolteacher and her son employed as an officer in a bank, *Mataji* had come to believe that her hardships would now be over. But then…. her son had fallen in love….with a colleague of his.

In a society where not only joint families but also the complex relations between mother-in-law and daughter-in-law are customary, being at loggerheads with each other most of the time is inevitable for both. No issue is required to pitch them against one another. Rather they are destined to be against each other. And so, issues need to be created. There's nothing unusual about it.

Mataji's son got married to *that* colleague, thus bringing in a competitor to his mother in the form of his wife. After that, both the mother and the wife were always in search of issues to fight about, and to demonstrate their superiority. When the situation became unbearable, then, with the mediation of relatives, the house was divided into two sections-one to be occupied by the son and his wife and the other to be occupied by that old lady-*Mataji* and *her loneliness.*

Mataji, who, till then had been struggling alone with her loneliness and illness, had now got a companion in Khatun, in front of whom she used to vent out her anger. And Khatun- she used to get sufficient material that kept her brain recharged with stories to be told in every household that she worked in.

"Nah. She was saying that she had to go out somewhere." Loveena replied standing on her terrace.

Hearing the voices Manju came out from her outhouse.

"But Babyji Khatun was standing near the shop. I had seen her when I went there to fetch milk an hour ago."

Now Loveena standing on the terrace, Manju outside her outhouse and that young boy at the gate- all three of them staring at each other blankly with the same thought crossing their minds- *Why had Khatun told a lie?*

Loveena for the first time felt herself sympathizing with *Mataji* whom she had never met but felt connected to through Khatun.

Khatun Begum had lost her parents when she was a kid. Having no siblings she was left behind all alone in this huge world. Some of her distant relatives had helped in her upbringing till she had become mature enough to look after herself, which was at quite an early age, as is with most of the orphaned children. She married, or more correctly, started living with an aged relative of hers who also died ten years after their *marriage* leaving behind her as a childless widow. After that, she was living all alone -this was the story of Khatun's life which everybody knew, although not directly from Khatun. Manju knew it from Loveena, Loveena from Mrs Reddy, Mrs Reddy knew it from her husband, and he knew it from the person in his office who had brought Khatun to him, and that person knew it from…. God knows who. But after that, nobody felt the need to stir this issue with Khatun. But Khatun gained everybody's sympathy.

"Khatun, where were you for the last two days?"

Two days had passed since Manju had told her that she had seen Khatun near the Sharma store and Khatun was missing from her work. *Mataji's* messenger was also appearing regularly at Loveena's gate enquiring about the maid's whereabouts.

Manju was in the kitchen and Loveena at the dining table busy with her breakfast when Khatun appeared at the door.

"Why? Hadn't I told you that I was going out of station for two days?"

Loveena felt as if Khatun's voice overflowing with surprise was banter to make her realize how forgetful she was.

"But Manju saw you near the Sharma store."

"How is that possible?" said Khatun moving her head sideways in denial, her widened eyes expressing shock and confusion. There was not a bit of fear in her voice on getting caught for her lie. For

Khatun, a gossipmonger, a mere word was enough to initiate a conversation or to weave a story around it and here Loveena had thrown a full sentence at her. Adjusting her *dupatta*, pulling up her *salwar* to her ankles she slowly lowered herself down on the floor resting her back against the wall.

Khatun was never in a hurry despite the amount of work she had committed herself to in Orchard Street. Whatever time she came in for work she would leave exactly an hour after her arrival. And the time she gossiped for was included in that hour. Gossiping was her birthright which she could not leave but she could and would leave behind the incomplete work beyond that designated hour. So Loveena sensed that today most of her cleaning work would be left undone.

"How is that possible?" repeated Khatun in a louder voice bringing Manju out of the kitchen.

"I had seen you." Now Manju was also there to prove her point.

"OH!" suddenly Khatun banged her forehead on the palm of her hand as if she had suddenly recalled something she had forgotten.

"Neither you nor I am wrong," said Khatun, a mysterious smile spreading on her lips, arousing confusion in Loveena and Manju's eyes.

"Khatun, how could you both be right? Stop this riddle and tell me whether you were there or not?" Loveena, whose eyes were moving continuously from the wall clock to Khatun's face was in no mood to linger on with this simple question.

"Manju must have seen my twin sister," Khatun's confidence and a loud guffaw following her answer softened both Loveena and Manju's faces, as both had realized what a fool they were for not having thought about this possibility.

It was only after a few days that Khatun's story of being all alone in the world without any siblings or anybody came back to Loveena's mind. She demanded clarification about it to which Khatun coldly summed up by saying that she didn't want to talk about her sister.

...So, either they were fools or Khatun was an excellent fabricator of stories.

MYSTERY RESOLVED

The Reddys had been living in Orchard Street for many years but the only thing that the harbinger of gossip Sharmaji knew about them was that Mr Reddy was a south Indian working as a scientist in the virology lab and in his family, he had a wife and two daughters. And if Sharmaji knew just this much about them, how could anybody else be expected to know anything more than that? But this was only till Khatun Begum arrived on the scene.

Sharmaji only knew that Khatun was hired for household work due to Mrs Reddy's crippling back injury endured by her sudden fall in the bathroom. *But the reason for the fall was still unknown.*

"How is Mrs Reddy now?"

"Not well. Restricted to her bed."

These few words exchanged between Khatun and Mrs Shastri, while arousing sympathy for that lesser-known poor woman on the one hand, added up to Mrs Shastri's agony on the other. The agony which, over a period of time, had become a part of her existence, settling permanently in her eyes, in the jowls, in the wrinkles on her forehead and in the twitching of her brow. Feeling her own helplessness resonating with Mrs Reddy's, she, in her measured steps, crossed that small distance to Mr Reddy's house, which was merely a house apart from that of their common neighbour the Harsimrans.

Just like a little warmth is enough to thaw the ice, similarly, one gesture of humanity is sufficient to germinate the seedling of trust.

Mrs Shastri was on her way to the *Sharma store* to buy groceries when she met Khatun and her steps deviated from *the Sharma store* to the Reddy household.

Mr Reddy had two daughters. The elder one was an engineer, married and settled in Bangalore, the *Silicon Valley of India*...the name again an extension of frustrated Indians' obsession with anything and everything foreign. The younger one was a doctor in the States.

Coming from a place where the name is prefixed with professional abbreviations and suffixed with the details of the degrees earned, these qualifications and abbreviations being displayed just like medals decorating the uniform of army officers. Having well-qualified daughters was a thing of envy for most of the people in their hometown, which was further magnified by the virtue of the younger one being a doctor and that too *abroad*. Where even the alterations in the prefixes and suffixes with the name were difficult to digest then what with the alteration of marital status? So, the day their younger daughter *informed* them of her getting married to a colleague of hers, an American, it was the day that created havoc in the life of the Reddy couple. How would their community react to it? They would now be disgraced by this act of their daughter. It would now provide an opportunity for their community to vent out their heartburn...was one of the many apprehensions that crossed their mind. And Mr Reddy.... He started cursing the moment in which he had decided to send his daughter abroad for studies and that also after taking a huge loan from the bank, cursed the moment in which she was born. As if all this cursing was not enough to soothe his agitation, he did that whose aftermath made him, in the end, curse himself for his habit of cursing.... he cursed Mrs Reddy for *her* upbringing of *their* daughter.

The minuscule virus whose molecular biology and biochemistry he was working on in his newly assigned project was also not exempted from his grumblings but Mrs Reddy who was living with him for the last thirty years had such an impact on him that he, despite his grumblings before her, had never dared to grumble *about her.*

The accusation that he made against his wife was more than enough to flare up Mrs Reddy's temper. Fear of society had an upper hand over his fear for his wife, making him adamant on his accusation. Now husband and wife were at loggerheads with each other. It was in one of those moments when the originating stress became intolerable for the poor lady making her unconscious and fall in the bathroom, hurting her back.

It was probably the first time in her life that Mrs Shastri had gotten hold of some information which was not known to anybody, neither Sharmaji nor Mr Shastri. And the anticipation of watching the transforming facial expressions while breaking this news that she was going to tell them, was giving her goosebumps, as it was for the first time in many years that she would be talking, and Mr Shastri would be listening to her. Life had always acted miserly with her while distributing the moments in which she could speak, neither when his newly born son was given a name nor when Mr Shastri, in a fit of rage, after knowing about his son's decision to settle abroad had banned his entry into the Shastri household. She was never given a chance to speak her mind but was only made to listen to the decisions taken by her husband. But today she was speaking out and Mr Shastri was listening.

But in the end, Mr Shastri again had the last laugh. "Poor Reddy. I always thought that bully Sherry to be the only challenger to Reddy's honour, but his daughter is also no less than that...Ah! Why only his daughter...your useless son is also just like it...challenging my honour and bringing disgrace to the family's name by abandoning his old parents."

Your son was often used sarcastically by Mr Shastri whenever he wanted to express his anger towards his son, but not without entangling his wife in lamentations despite there being no fault of hers. *Their* son had decided to settle abroad and Mr Shastri was against the decision. She was nowhere in the scene. But afterwards, it was only she who used to bear the brunt of his anger. Many years had passed since their son had visited them, occasionally speaking to his mother on the telephone. Mrs Shastri got accustomed to this blabbering but today her husband's words stunned her for a moment.

"How could you compare our son with Sherry...a dog?"

"Why not? Both the species are unpredictable in their behaviour... always ready to scare you, to attack you," blurted out Mr Shastri while pouring out a drink for himself, something that he immensely enjoyed.

Mr Shastri, enjoying his drink suddenly felt a sense of amusement at his comparison.

"Haha...Sherry...your son...haha..."

The storyteller Mr Shastri, the loquacious Harsimran and the always grumbling Mr Reddy, despite the diversities and variations in their characters, had certain chords of life that were common to all of them, emanating the same music when plucked.

Loveena, after enduring her problems and chaos, had developed sensitivity towards the surge of other people's underlying emotions. It was this sensitivity or acknowledgement that made her make Mrs Reddy, who was on the road to recovery, overcome her miseries.

With settling down of the ashen fog of despondency started the settling down of regrets, thus resulting in the emergence of that guilelessness which she was born with. It expressed itself in the gleam and joy of her almond-shaped eyes. *Whether it is the experience of life or from life, the impressions left behind are everlasting.* Loveena's experiences were secured safely in the depths of her heart. This accumulated treasure heightened her faculties, making her rightly judge the unspoken sentiments of any person she faced. When she faced a crippled Mrs Reddy, she acknowledged the pain Mrs Reddy was enduring at that moment. Her distress was both physical and mental. She understood a mother's agony arising out of her fears regarding her daughter's future. Loveena felt that pain because she had already endured that phase with her mother. She could very well feel the intensity and texture of that feeling, making her sensitive towards Mrs Reddy. This understanding was enough to develop an instant bond with her.

Loveena's comforting words pacified Mrs Reddy's agitated heart. "Don't allow baseless fears to overpower yourself. Try to imagine your daughter's happiness. Recall how happy you were at the time of your wedding. Your daughter is also passing through that same phase of her life now. Immerse yourself in her happiness..."

Mrs Reddy, who earlier felt herself bereft of all the enthusiasm, now got a new dimension, a new perspective on the happenings of life through Loveena's words, bringing in her a sense of not only emotional but also physical well-being. With this, the physical body being merely a reflection of the emotional self also sets on the path to recovery.

As the weeks passed so was the tide of distress but *only to be followed by another.*

After making peace with the thought of having a foreigner, an American son-in-law they started feeling proud of having a foreigner as a family member -fair-skinned and blond. Probably blue-eyed also...but they were not certain in this aspect. Their daughter had not yet sent them his photograph as she wanted to introduce him to her parents in person. Crazy girl!

The only things they were familiar with about him were his name and occupation -Dr James. The day the couple formalized their relationship in the presence of a few friends in a court somewhere in the States, the Reddy couple congratulated them, thus becoming a long-distance witness to their daughter's wedding. In their brief chat with James over the telephone, Mr Reddy felt like a fool, able to utter only monosyllables without understanding a word of what James had spoken. And Mrs Reddy, she on seeing the flushed expression on her husband's face, feared to even hold the receiver. The first encounter -traumatic, dogmatic and emphatic.

When the happenings of life are not in tandem with the desires of the heart, then the brain is always occupied with proving that what has happened is better than what was desired. The two halves of Mr Reddy's brain were also most of the time at loggerheads with each other with two contradictory thoughts. One half which was still battling with the embarrassment of acting like a fool on the telephone and was not ready to accept James, and the other one, the more practical one, which understood the uselessness of resistance to the decision that had already been taken, providing him with the reasons to feel proud of having James as his son-in-law. This conflict was something too big for the size of his brain. So, with a conflict always going on between these two halves, he himself merely acted like a spectator. He was always engrossed in this conflict to such an extent that instead of observing his surroundings he visualized the conflict within, and instead of hearing the external sounds he

          MYSTERY RESOLVED

was busy listening to the catechism and cross-questioning between those two never tiring halves of his brain.

It was probably in one of those moments that while coming from the office that an incident took place which blasted not only the unperturbed silence of the mountains but also the acridity among the neighbours. Before anybody could understand anything, the scene unfolded in front of the *Sharma store*. Mr Reddy was spread on the road with Harsimran, with his outstretched hands covering Mr Reddy like a blanket. Sherry was standing on one side gnawing his teeth with anger.

Khatun Begum, who was going back after doing her work for the day at Orchard Street was the lone witness and thus the lone narrator of the incident.

"I was just a few meters away from *Sharma store* when I saw a lost Mr Reddy coming back from his office. Harsimran was gossiping with Sharmaji, and an unleashed Sherry was standing on one side of the road, with his rear towards an approaching Mr Reddy. Mr Reddy was so lost in his thoughts that he failed to notice that burly Sherry. As I raised an alarm, Harsimran, *the saviour*, jumped in."

Harsimran, a little far off from the unleashed Sherry, was standing on that narrow-metalled road and had noticed a lost Mr Reddy coming towards Sherry who was standing with his rear towards him. Anticipating the outcome, in a blink of an eye when Mr Reddy crashed upon Sherry, at that very moment Harsimran jumped over Mr Reddy in an effort to protect him from Sherry. Sherry's growl, Mr Reddy's cry and Harsimran's shriek all got mingled together creating a momentary furore.

Harsimran who was earlier always critical of Mr Reddy, after coming to know about his daughter's marriage with a foreigner, had developed a newfound respect for him. After all, Harsimran came from a community where the only purpose of taking birth in this world is to go to Canada or America or England...or anywhere on this earth but away from India.

"Sherry," roared Harsimran, "you useless creature. Never dare to attack Reddyji again." Sherry growled looking angrily towards Mr Reddy as if to say *it was not me but Mr Reddy who attacked me.*

It was the first time that Sherry got scolded and that too for no fault of his. Mr Reddy's eyes widened in surprise. And that was the day when Harsimran smiled at Mr Reddy, and he also smiled back. It was an incident that Mr Reddy did not want to become public but with Khatun the witness it not only became known to the residents of Orchard Street but also to Mr Reddy's office staff. And it was also the incident which publicized Harsimran as *the saviour.*

   MYSTERY RESOLVED

AWAKENING

The matrix of Loveena's life, after getting ingrained with the diversity of relations at Orchard Street, had started adorning itself with bright hues of rainbow. This inner beautification radiated in an exuberance in her aura. The world, with its magic and beauty, now seemed inviting to her, ready to embrace her and reveal its beauty and treasure of hidden wisdom. The day she sauntered out of the confines of Orchard Street bypassing that small shop, Sharma general store, on the tarred road leading to the small town of Banikhet, she felt enchanted by everything that her eyes could get sight of. She felt charmed walking on that empty tarred road cutting through dense forests, stopping occasionally to imbibe the overflowing nectar of peace all around. She stood spellbound in front of the *Dak bungalow*. The wooden structure imbuing its Victorian-era charm seemed to be oblivious to the fact that its masters had long left the place. It made Loveena visualize the past when it was inhabited by the English. And so, piercing the thick wall of the time spanning many decades, she jumped into the past to listen to the whines and gallops of the horses, imagining officers in their starched uniforms, madams in their delicately embroidered gowns and broad-brimmed hats, children with their governesses, uniformed orderlies, who comprised of the local people, waiting upon them. The awe in the eyes of those uniformed orderlies that she was imagining standing in front of the *Dak Bungalow*, she realized was still intact in the minds of the present generation even after so many decades of the colonial masters having left the country. And she kept on walking downhill feeling joyous at everything...or in actuality *with herself.*

The small hill town of Banikhet had everything that was required for sustenance. And it was here only that Loveena realized how little was actually required for it.

After climbing down the tarred road for a few kilometers she had now reached the heart of Banikhet which consisted of a small market complex called Indira market, a dispensary and a secondary school. The market complex had all the necessary shops...*Harsimran's shop must also be somewhere in this market only*, she thought. Across the market complex, after climbing down about fifty stairs, was a small temple. Climbing down those stairs Loveena found herself in the well-kempt cemented verandah of a temple. The serenity provided by the surrounding forest was only heightened by the musical sound of a stream flowing nearby, that must have descended somewhere from the heights of the snow-clad mountains. The golden yellow of the bright sun blended perfectly with the clear blue of the gushing stream making it radiate like a crystal...pure and delicate. Cemented steps, albeit giving a glimpse of the underlying bricks with their wearied-out cement falling apart, facilitated devotees to reach that stream sprinkled with the purity and humility of the magnificent mountains.

From counting the rooms of *the haveli* and the houses in Orchard Street to now counting those stairs outside the temple...Loveena counted five steps- yes, they were five in number. Sitting on the lowermost step she lowered her feet into the cold waters making her experience a sudden surge of shiver along her spine. The penetrating rays of the bright afternoon sun soon nullified the chilling impact of the cold water making her feel comfortable.

"Ah! Today I am a guest at God's house." The emergence of this thought gave birth to a train of thoughts. The surrounding dense forests, the sun shining in its full glory, the gushing water of the stream exhibiting its fierceness, the gently blowing cool breeze ruffling her curly hair -everything made her believe that God, sitting comfortably inside the temple, was busy crafting out all these embellishments to balm the restless souls. These thoughts brought a contented smile to her lips.

She remembered the last time she had come here along with her parents...many years ago. If one measures time in numbers, then decades seem to be a long time back but if one tries to measure it in terms of memories then it just seems to be a matter of yesterday... so near that it could be touched by merely extending one's hand. Sitting there Loveena also felt that memory to be so close to her heart and so clear to her eyes that she could detail it out completely. She recalled the pink dress she was wearing that day; she recalled her stubbornness to not walk making her father carry her on his shoulders, she recalled how her mother made her meet the priest of the temple and made her touch his feet to get his blessings... she recalled everything. The calming thoughts and the memories made her get connected with the place, which was enough for a reason to come back to the place again and again.

Despite the outer structure of the temple being well in its senectitude, its inner sanctum having white marble idols was well maintained. It was the oldest and only temple of the town, having seen the rise and fall of many decades...or centuries, having not only folk tales associated with it but also the faith of people. Loveena, who till her youth, had never felt the need for God and who after the calling off of her engagement with Sanand and other incidents in her life, had rather developed a strong revulsion for Him, for her faith had become something unacceptable. But now, sitting on the steps of the temple, she felt that aversion getting diluted by that gushing water and she developed an instant liking for the place.

After sitting there undisturbed for a long time, she saw an elderly man, an ascetic, with a *kamandal* standing behind her. The ribcage on his bare torso was clearly visible beneath his flimsy sheet of skin.

The only cloth on his body was a loin cloth wrapped tightly around his waist. His matted white hair wrapped into a bun overweighed the small head that they were resting upon. The beard touching his chest was also stiffened with dust and grime. His taut skin, devoid of any underlying fat, was incapable of displaying emotions or even the wrinkles corresponding to his age. The only thing that hypnotized Loveena were his eyes. Eyes so clear and pure like the water of the stream.

Baba.

Loveena touched his feet.

Neither the age of the temple nor that of the ascetic was known to anybody. The ascetic was the constant of the temple whereas the other person, the priest who was appointed by the temple trust kept on changing. The trust was comprised of four members who were selected from the applicants based on the financial contribution they could make towards the kitty of the temple. The more the contribution, the higher the chance of an appointment. These used to be the influential people of that small town. The desperation to be a member of the trust was not due to religious propensities but political ones- because of the chairman of the trust. The chairman always used to be the local politician and by becoming a member of the trust, it was easy to gain his confidence. In a society where Darwin's theory of *survival of the fittest* had been aptly modified into *the survival of the politically associated*, such association with trust was an effort in that direction.

But leaving aside all the objectives of the trust, the priest was an employee of the trust who was getting paid for managing the affairs and looking after the maintenance of that temple. He was an employee and he behaved like one. The small two-roomed accommodation behind the temple was the house allotted to him

       AWAKENING

where he lived with his family. Besides drawing salary in lieu of his services towards God he used to perform religious rituals at local residents' places in his personal capacity.

Contrary to the lifestyle of the priest, the ascetic most of the time was withdrawn within himself undistracted by the worldly chaos. Many times, his sitting motionless for long periods, made people mistake him for dead but even then, nobody ever dared to disturb him. His requirements were meagre-a loin cloth to cover his body and a piece of fruit every two or three days to fill his stomach. With no other requirements, he hardly had ever felt the need to leave the confines of that temple. *Very few were the occasions when he had talked to anybody. But whenever he talked, his words were full of wisdom penetrating the shallowness of worldly illusions and reaching the depths of the soul of the listener. His discourse was considered to be so empowering that it could change the direction of one's life. Blessed were the souls who got a chance to listen to him* –these were the talks which kept circulating amongst the people. Many people talked about it, but nobody had ever been a witness to this.

Loveena, getting obsessed with the place, had become devout and started frequenting it. She had never heard the ascetic speak, but always felt his aura full of peace and tranquility. She used to come and sit on the verandah of the temple, the corner of which was occupied by that ascetic. Most of the time he was sitting with his eyes closed.

Neither the ascetic was looking for a disciple, nor had Loveena ever thought of becoming one, but then the incidents which have the power to change the course of life's direction are always unexpected and unthought of.

"You can experience the rumbling of stream, the gushing of wind, the fierceness of fire, the vastness of the sky and the strength of earth within you. The human body itself is a combination of these *panchtatva* created by Him. You have all these within you, and you can feel them."

Baba's words in a deep and clear voice were nothing less than a jolt bringing Loveena, who was sitting on the steps leading to the stream, out of her slumber. She was so engrossed in her thoughts that she had failed to notice *Baba* standing quietly behind her. Turning swiftly with curiosity, she found herself at a loss for words. And before Loveena could comprehend anything, she found the ascetic lowering his *kamandal* into the stream to fill it with water. Then while climbing up the steps to the temple he uttered a few more words without looking towards Loveena.

"Surrender yourself to trust and faith."

Baba's voice had a conviction, a strength and a command...*to have faith and to get rid of distrust.*

It was the first time since Loveena had started coming to the temple that that *Baba* had said something to her. Just the way raindrops are readily absorbed by parched earth to quench its thirst or to merge themselves completely with the texture of the earth, similarly *Baba's* words were also readily soaked in by her soul, becoming one with it.

"Isn't it true that I don't have trust in anybody? Isn't it true that I have always taken the world to be a *menacing place*? Was *Ma* wrong in telling me this? But how could trust be generated when everybody is ready to stab you in the back...to hurt you?" *Baba's* words made her ponder over several doubts arising within her. And these doubts were not without reason...she was not born with them but was made to learn them, to practice them while growing up.

With Loveena hesitatingly and silently following him, *Baba* returned to his place- the corner in the verandah of the temple. With Baba closing his eyes and retracting into his inner world, she

 AWAKENING

kept sitting there for a long time after that, in the hope of getting more answers from him.

Baba had shown her the way - to have trust and faith in Him and His creation.

The layer of this worldly attribute was too thick to be dissolved in a moment, but it was in that moment that that thick layer got jolted up, got somewhat loosened and shredded a few of its fragments. It was a beginning. After that, many months had passed and Loveena kept on visiting the temple regularly in the hope of listening to something more from the ascetic. She would come in the morning and would sit through the afternoon, only to return back to her home in disappointment. But the tranquility of the place, a desire to understand life in the light of *Baba's* words got kindled in her heart.

"*Samadhi* is the zenith of meditation. It is only when one reaches that state then consciousness, which is a slave of ever-wavering thoughts, starts mastering those thoughts ultimately silencing them. With it starts emerging the stillness of soul adamantine enough not to be penetrated by the chaos of the outer world."

Taking a slow and deep inhalation *Baba* seemed to get lost somewhere with an intent gaze fixed on Loveena that was not looking at her but was looking through her, somewhere beyond-beyond everything, into the very source of the emergence of the whole creation. The deep chasm that was visible in the gleam of his pure and glinting eyes made Loveena believe that *Baba* was looking at something which was securely hidden from the human eye- truth beneath the illusions of human existence. After a silence of a few moments, as if searching for the right words to deliver the profundity of the experiences that he had endured throughout his life in a nutshell to Loveena, *Baba* continued, "Once attained, this rock-hard stillness of the soul engulfs all the sensuous awareness. The only feeling left behind is the awareness of the cosmic energy entering and leaving the body with every inhalation and exhalation. In that moment, the body also ceases to exist resulting in the visualization of the oneness of the inner and outer energy. This is *samadhi,* and when this stage is attained, one becomes a part of the grand music of universe which is continuously emitting from the *damru* of Lord Shiva, the eternal sound of *Aum* giving meaning to the nothingness of this whole universe."

Baba's words left Loveena in profound contemplation. She was not merely listening to but was experiencing those words. She felt as if the words were gently peeling off the layers of darkness, the layers of ignorance wrapping around her soul, revealing its brilliance. And as those words were trickling into her soul bit by bit, becoming a part of it, she felt blissful.

Baba took a deep breath and before closing his eyes again murmured in a faint sound, "*Aum* the genesis and *Aum* the ending of life... with everything in between occupied with a desire to decipher and to understand it."

"*Aum...Aum...*"

The words slipping effortlessly from the mouth of the ascetic with the fluttering of his thin and flaky lips partially hidden beneath his beard were nothing less than pearls of wisdom. Loveena was sitting spellbound. Save for her, the only other person in the audience, the portly priest... afternoon being the time when there were no devotees, he was sleeping peacefully in a corner on the mat.

 AWAKENING

"People come here, bow before me and believe me to have some magical powers."

"But aren't they right in believing so? Otherwise, how could one endure hunger and the adversities of this climate? You don't eat, you don't protect yourself from the harshness of the weather...then how are you surviving? Isn't it some magic?" Loveena, who was accustomed only to listening to *Baba's* sermons without gathering courage to hinder the smooth flow of his wonderful words, for the first time questioned him.

"Hmm...It is not magic. It is complete surrender."

The old ascetic's momentary silence after the sentence made Loveena anxious for him to continue with the discourse. But she also knew that it was only on an impulse that that old man ever spoke anything. He spoke only when he felt like speaking, suddenly withdrawing himself amidst a talk. But today Loveena also wanted to know more and maybe *Baba* had understood that.

"It is not magic. It is *something* every one of us is born with but start losing it as we start losing trust. I told you that the creator had created everything using the same raw material. We have all the components of this universe within us. We have heat, light, air, earth and sky within. But not every one of us has retained that unquestionable trust in Him that every one of us was inherently born with. And I have that unfailing trust in Him and his creation. When people watch me sitting in the cold, then it is because the fire or the heat within keeps me warm and when you see me sitting in the heat, then it is the air within that keeps me comfortable. And when I read other people's minds, it is also not magic. When the whole universe is within then anything happening anywhere in the world is happening within and I just have to close my eyes to see within."

Baba's words again gave a new dimension to Loveena's thoughts. She noticed *Baba* closing his eyes -an indication that it was more than enough for him to tell her and still more for her to imbibe.

It was the last time that she had seen him. A few days after the meeting she heard about the ascetic's disappearance from the temple. His followers tried to search for him but without any success.

"There was a very strong gush of wind over the temple after which I have not found him anywhere. It seems as if he was flown away with the wind," the priest was telling people. Most of them laughed at him, with very few believing him. But Loveena was one of those few. Besides believing that portly priest, one more thing that Loveena believed in was that *baba* was there only to guide her through her life's journey and to make her realize that life was neither as difficult as she was made to believe nor so bad as to retract from it-but that is only when you surrender yourself completely to Him.

"Surrender yourself to faith and trust. If you believe and trust that the elements surrounding you are the same as the elements within then ...then *isn't it possible for them to merge into each other."*

Baba's words echoed in Loveena's ears and the faith and trust in the world or *samsara* that she had lost during her life's journey rerooted itself firmly into her soul, crumbling and demolishing the thick layered wall of fears and negativities deposited within. With the clearing up of the debris started the wiping away of the darkness and restlessness of her soul leaving behind the brilliance in which started to germinate a desire to take a deep plunge in this *samsara* in order to understand it and to appreciate it. It is only by taking a deep plunge into the illusions of *samsara* one can experience the bliss hidden beneath. The mesmerizing thing is that this journey is two-way -the deeper one plunges into *samsara*, the deeper the inward plunge will be. While experiencing the bliss hidden beneath this universe one experiences the bliss hidden within.

The merger of the outer and the inner energy-The ultimate and profound wisdom. All the beauty and purity is to indulge in and not to withdraw from.

AN EXALTATION

The welcoming warmth and brightness of the sun, offsetting the morning chill calmly and leisurely stepped into the frosty evenings, imparting a soporific texture to the environment, enveloping everything within it. Wistful for restless souls and blissful for tranquil ones. The drowsiness of the climate had also steadily seeped into the lives of the people living on Orchard Street, making it worthless to keep track of the passing days. And each day slid smoothly, revealing the next one underneath, which most of the time used to be identical to the previous one as if it had merely refreshed itself. In the past five years, it was the first time that Loveena was experiencing an enthusiasm for becoming part of some celebration. Four months had passed since the episode of the wedding of Mr Reddy's daughter. Mrs Reddy had recuperated from her injury, but Khatun was still there.

The conundrum of human behaviour is hard to decipher. Desire to be a global citizen, desire to be familiar with different cultures and languages, desire to have transnational professional contacts –but everything fuzzes out at the very prospect of having transnational family relations. The truth is that however fast the world seems to be changing, the human mind is lagging far behind in its adaptation to those changes. The same was the case for the Reddy couple, who by now had attained some success in accepting the truth and making peace with themselves. But still, to break the news of this wedding to their community in their hometown had not been an easy task for them. But now, their newly married daughter was coming to visit them with her husband. Then how could a wedding be celebrated without a gathering? And how could a gathering be possible without relatives and friends?

The series of events of the past few months that chanced upon in the lives of the residents jolted them out of their slumber ensuing an affinity among them. The sluggish days gained momentum. Now every passing day started expressing a new shade of life. The Reddy couple, Harsimrans, Shastri couple and Loveena -sitting on chairs forming a circle in Mr Shastri's lawn absorbed in discussions became a daily ritual or more rightly the only ritual of the day that they longed for. The time of arrival of the newlyweds was swiftly approaching, but still, an acceptable and respectable way to celebrate the wedding had not been worked out yet.

"Receive the newlyweds in your hometown along with your relatives. That's the only customary way." Harsimran, the wife's suggestion in a confused voice was enough to aggravate Mr Reddy's anxiety.

"Relatives...Huh! Relatives....they are...Hmm...they are worse than... than.... yes, worse than ...Sherry." Mr Reddy's comparison in an anxious and stammered rumbling surprised everyone...and most of all Mrs Shastri.

"Is Sherry the epitome of troubles? How could anybody compare these two different species...."

Mrs Shastri's hysterical ranting with her intent gaze fixed on her husband's face was enough to arouse a plethora of thoughts in the minds of that small gathering.

"Oh! Such a love for our Sherry." Harsimran, the wife thought.

"Reddyji, why are you dragging my Sherry in your trouble?" questioned Harsimran, the husband in a confused voice.

"Why is Mrs Shastri staring angrily at Mr Shastri for a statement made by Reddyji?" Loveena thought to herself.

Mr Shastri, for the first time in his life, felt intimidated by his frail and fragile wife.

"You crazy woman! Why are you overreacting?" Mr Shastri, in an effort to hold on to the losing ground, began scolding his wife when Mrs Reddy interrupted him.

"Nah... Meeting them for the first time in front of so many relatives isn't acceptable to me," muttered Mrs Reddy, oblivious to the happenings around her, perspiring at the very thought of meeting the newlyweds in front of her relatives. Tiny beads of sweat appeared on her forehead enough to wipe away the aggression of the moment only to replace it with sympathy for the poor woman.

"You nasty fellow. Why are you sitting here listening to our talk?" Mr Shastri's sudden and high-pitched roar at the very sight of Palaram sitting near a flower bed frightened everybody.... including Mrs Shastri.

Neither Mr Shastri, whose mind wavered with the drop of a needle, nor Harsimran who was still battling with his anxiety at the prospect of meeting a foreigner in Orchard Street, was able to provide Mr Reddy with a desirable way out from his dilemma. And Mrs Shastri maintained her silence for fear of getting silenced and lambasted by her husband in front of so many people. Passing of time and getting no solution to the problem were adding to the cursing of Mr Reddy. Mrs Reddy was the one who was now sitting there silently and nervously, her anxiety being clearly reflected in her furrowed brows and curled-up lips.

"Why not organize a small get-together here to welcome the newlyweds on their arrival? After getting comfortable with your son-in-law, you can proceed with a reception in your hometown, breaking the news of the wedding to your people."

Loveena's words silenced them all. Mrs Reddy raised her brows, now relaxing the curled-up lip and Mr Reddy nodded putting an end to his cursing.

The colourful tent with small bells attached to its ruffles was creating a dulcet jingling music while swaying slowly under the impact of the gentle breeze.

"Is the fine music, which Ramchand had mentioned about, in the stillness of nights sweeter than this sound?... But he had told that that music could only be heard with the silencing of inner chaos...the music from the *damru* of Lord Shiva transcending down from the steepness of those sky touching mountains, the abode of Lord Shiva...," standing in Mr Reddy's lawn, with her gaze fixed somewhere in infinity, a number of thoughts were crossing Loveena's mind like clouds. She, after partaking in her share of vintages from the simmering pot of life, was on her way towards settling down of her inner chaos. She had started realizing that ever existing inner babel is the only source of muddling the arising thoughts. The incidents of the past, apprehensions regarding the future...are the fountainhead of the babels, the restlessness and they can neither be settled down by forgiving nor by forgetting anything but only by *acceptance*. With acceptance settles down all the muck, all the confusion making every thought, every fear redundant, creating peace within. And this acceptance could only be attained by drenching oneself fully in each and every flavour of life, feeling it to the core till there is left behind no desire to have more of it. Then only one knows and hence accepts that that taste existed but he neither laments its existence nor wants to take or give more of it to anybody. Then one also starts understanding the dilemmas of another person- the one who is undergoing that state of mind- making one give away the aggressiveness of reactions thus making him more humane. All the wisdom which had started to reveal itself to her had a calming impact on her but *maybe was still insufficient to make her listen to that fine music.* Her beautiful face beamed under the brilliance of a smile that radiated only peace, gratitude and joy.

A sudden blare of jarring music engulfed the delicate jingling of bells bringing Loveena out of her thoughts. The technician was setting up his audio equipment. Caterers were putting up tables, covering them with white tablecloth. Some workers from the tent house were unloading plastic chairs from a tempo. Floral decorations along the path to Mr Reddy's house starting from *Sharma store*, red- and yellow-coloured plastic chairs, tables with neat tablecloth, multi- coloured tent in the backdrop, foot tapping Bollywood Hindi songs-all set in Mr Reddy's lawn, everything was exuding joy and eagerness to welcome the newlyweds.

It was Harsimran who exhibited his sound business skills while taking charge of every preparation. The tent house owner, being a friend of his provided them with the most colourful and fancy tent and bright coloured chairs of the latest design from his tent shop -which he had kept apart for his distinguished customers. Further, in his anxiety to impress James, he had brought a good caterer from the adjoining town who was good at cooking continental food, and a floral designer to decorate that small street was brought in from Pathankot. His enthusiasm to leave a mark on James's memory regarding preparations was infectious, enveloping everyone in its fervour.

Mr Reddy wanted to surprise his daughter with an unexpected welcome party, their daughter wanted to surprise her parents by introducing them to their son-in-law for the first time ...and life wanted to surprise them all.

The progressing evening stirred up the place with a magic wand, filling it up with the clinking and clattering of utensils, riffs and lyrics of melodious Hindi songs, smoke arising out from burning

     AN EXALTATION

coal and aroma of food, anxiety emanating from tensed-up Reddy couple and chattering of that small gathering of residents of Orchard street-everything was illuminated with the strings of multi- coloured lights and white bulbs dangling from every tree and shrub in the lawn and along the path to the Reddy household.

Loveena, sitting on a chair near Mrs Shastri, with her thoughts swinging between the present and the past, sensed a similarity between the anxiety of her mother and that of Mrs Reddy. Her mother was anxious for her then, and now Mrs Reddy was anxious for her daughter. She knew how agonizing the feeling was. And with this knowledge, she understood Mrs Reddy's worries even without communicating with her. Suddenly she felt a gush of air against her skin making her shiver.

"Ah! How could anybody call this month to be a summer month in the hills?"

Loveena's words brought a smile to Mrs Shastri's wrinkled face.

"Climate of the hills is static-always cold. It never changes its character, unlike human beings."

Loveena felt as if the sounds, the aromas which were earlier slowly spreading in every nook and corner like water pouring out slowly from an outlet, had all suddenly stopped spreading due to the closure of that outlet, choking everybody and especially the Reddy couple -with Mrs Reddy gasping for breath and Mr Reddy getting held by Mr Shastri before falling down.

The sound of a car horn reaching Orchard Street way before its arrival alerted everybody. After landing at the Delhi International Airport, the couple had hired a taxi to reach Banikhet. Homecomings are usually the most awaited occasions and so was it for the Reddys, but the only difference was that that the joyous wait was corrupted by the feelings of anxiety and nervousness. But the moment they faced each other the anxieties expanded, engulfing all the little bits of joy present in that moment. Opening the door of that bulky ambassador, Mr Reddy's daughter dressed up in denim and a loose top alighted from the car, followed by her husband. There stood behind her a tall man of a height which nobody in Orchard Street could dare to match, not even Harsimran with his six feet body frame. But it was not his height that sent shivers down the spine of the parents ...but his complexion, which was so dark that it appeared to blend with the darkness of moonless night, making the white of his eyes the only thing that was shining brilliantly. At that very moment the DJ, exhibiting his professional skills, welcoming the newlyweds and desirous of making the moment memorable, raised the volume of music. *Music also has the power to fill in the void created by unexpected shocks.*

"You had told us that you have married an American," mumbled Mr Reddy with helplessness oozing from his every word.

"Sherry...I apologize. Ah! Your species is much better." Mr Shastri's muttering, which was nothing more than a whisper caught hold of his wife's ears attracting a lost look from her.

Belonging to a country where people still find pride in being associated with the things synonymous with the British, even after so many decades of them having left the country, be it their name or the colour of their skin. So, for most of the people who had taken it for granted for an American to be a fair-complexioned man with blond hair, the dark complexion was nothing less than a thunderbolt. It was this sudden shock from the unexpected turn of events that became intolerable for the poor parents.

     AN EXALTATION

DIN AMIDST MIDNIGHT

With the string of mountains, with their ice-capped peaks, appearing like pearls in a necklace, surrounding it, that tiny habitation was settled comfortably in their lap. The secretive hidden and absolute silence of those mountains rode the rays of the sun and captured every atom of air, making its presence felt in every nook and corner of the valley. This unworldly silence, while devoid of all shades itself, reflects all shades of the human mind on it, leading it to be categorized sometimes as peaceful, sometimes as tranquil and sometimes as maddening. *But when this silence trickles into the minds and hearts of the people, overriding their ranting and logic, then it starts reverberating with the eternal silence of the soul. And then this silence can be anything but maddening.*

The chirping of birds, gibbering of troops of monkeys passing by or the rare sawing roar of a leopard roaming in the wild, pierce through the stiffness of this quiet only to make it more thumping, more resounding. But silence is also communicative, having a language of its own. Loveena, over a period of time, after getting acclimatized not only to life but also to the quiet of the hills, had developed a keen ear for the faintest of stirrings being emitted into this profound silence. With her eyes closed and her senses directed towards the faintest sound, she would try to decipher its source, the conversation or message or emotions beneath it, making her feel and understand it. She felt these sounds cognate with the beating human heart.

A beating human heart symbolizes life in a body, similarly, the sounds of nature symbolize life in it.

The panic-stricken voices and cries that awakened her amidst that peaceful night were enough to affright her, making her heart hammer heavily in her chest. Confusion in thoughts on being jolted out from a deep sleep, a heart pounding fiercely, and a sudden rush of adrenaline making her swelter even on that cold night -all this numbed her brain for a moment. But soon gaining back control of herself, she sat in her bed and wiped off the tiny beads of perspiration from her forehead with the back of her hands. Clutching the shawl lying on the nearby chair she rushed towards the terrace to get a glimpse of what had happened.

The thicket of the darkness of the cold night obscuring the silver of the moon beneath it was preventing her vision from penetrating through. The branches of the huge tree near the entrance of her gate were also obstructing the clear view of the happenings on the road. She turned her head only to get a glimpse of the far-off pine trees which seemed to get melted into that darkness leaving behind a darker imprint on the canvas of the night, and whose presence could be made out only by their faint silhouette. Their gentle and slight swaying gave them a monstrous appearance dreading Loveena. The stillness appeared frightful, adding to her anxiety, making her abruptly turn off all her imaginations and focus her gaze intently towards Ramchand's house. The faint yellow of his kitchen bulb scattering through the glass pane of the kitchen window made her notice the open door of his house making it clear that they were also not inside. She sensed some movement in the street but could not make anything out of it. Wrapping the shawl tightly around her shoulders she rushed downstairs.

On coming out in the street she found Manju and Ramchand standing amidst a small crowd in front of Harsimran's house encircling Mrs Reddy. Inching closer, she found the Harsimrans, Shastris and Palaram standing there.

     DIN AMIDST MIDNIGHT

The rawness of nature, unblemished by human intrusions, has nothing to perturb the peace of mind, rather it is the other way round –the perturbed mind has a lot of energy to disturb the peace of nature. Many months had passed since that fateful night when the Reddys had thrown the party to welcome the newlyweds, but not without rooting itself in the form of an unforgiving anger towards their daughter, which had manifested itself in the form of fears and anxieties in them. Mrs Reddy had somewhat accepted the situation but Mr Reddy, failing to come to terms with it, had become more confused, more frustrated and often behaved in a moronic manner. After that day, the darkness of the night had become a nightmare for him. The darkness of the nights, the darkness of James's complexion and the darkness of Mr Reddy's thoughts...darkness had enveloped his whole self, making his life miserable. And that day also it was this darkness that had seeped into his dreams, becoming the reason behind stirring the calm environment with hysterical sounds, frightening the neighbours.

He dreamed and the dream was about his grandchildren. He had dreamed them to be born with the same darkness that he was now scared of, of this darkness superimposing with the dark of the night, making it hard for him to even make out their silhouette, except for the white of their eyes that shone like bulbs, making him sit abruptly in his bed gasping for breath. Then he experienced an intense tightening in his chest with its excruciating pain spreading along his shoulders and the arm and this was enough for his poor wife to panic. At this time of midnight, failing to understand what to do, she had rushed out into the street and cried out for help, bringing out all the neighbours. With emergency health services many kilometers away from that small locality, Harsimran had rushed to bring in a doctor known to him, who was residing in the town.

Loveena all of a sudden recalled the trauma she had herself endured several times- when Sanand's family had called off their engagement, after her parents' demise or after realizing her folly of marrying Vikram and many other times...whenever she felt her anxieties overpowering her. She felt as if she herself was experiencing the pain arising in Mr Reddy's chest and in that moment, she believed it to be the same panic attack that her doctor had once told her about. She rushed back to bring the medicines that she had always kept with her, but now seldom used as with her self- realization her chaotic self was slowly disappearing. By the time Harsimran had come in with the doctor, Mr Reddy was already sleeping comfortably.

While going towards her house, a soft gentle and cold sensation on her cheek made her lift up her eyes, only to get a glimpse into the pristine beauty of the darkness which had started showering her with divine love in the form of tiny, powdery and cold white flakes of snow.

 DIN AMIDST MIDNIGHT

THE REALIZATION

Endowed with sufficient resources to lead a comfortable life but devoid of extravagant claims, crimes were seldom committed in Banikhet, and absolutely never in the isolated habitation of Orchard Street. The absence of crime and the peaceful coexistence of the community were adequate reasons for the hibernation of the police department of this town. The puniness of the department was clearly reflected in its single-room office which housed the police station. It was located in the heart of the town, close to the market complex near the temple. Fear of God in the *afterlife* and fear of law *in this life* -blinkers to the notorious human mind.

In the police station were deputed merely two people -one an ASI and the other one his subordinate, a constable. The condition of the police station, with its discoloured damp walls and shabby but ponderous furniture, was as pathetic as its occupants.

They must have heavily bribed the selection committee... was the only thought and probably the rightful one also in the minds of all the people who ever came across the two policemen. Their thin frail structures covered in oversized uniforms made them appear to be struggling inside it to protect themselves from getting lost in that huge garment. The flapped chest pocket on one half of the sagging shirt was enough to cover a major part of the chest and their loose trousers were held in place by broad leather belts, but not without forming pleats on the backside.

It was the constable's responsibility to unlock the police station in the morning. And once after opening it, they would disappear only to return back at the time of closing it. The only thing that made people have a bit of confidence in them was the revolver hanging on their delicate waists. A motorcycle was provided to them by their department, the heavy body of which seemed like torture for their lean frames to control.

Their jurisdiction remained confined to the market square. That was until that day when riding on that big bulky motorcycle, they appeared in Orchard Street. In a place which, with its profound silence, would get disturbed by even a sneeze, the heavy sound of the bike climbing uphill was more than enough to announce their arrival. It attracted the residents, mostly the domestic helps, to the road, with everyone throwing curious glances their way, and then speeding back into their houses to break the news to their masters. Before they had even entered Orchard Street the news of their arrival had spread in every nook and corner like a forest fire.

"What happened?... What has gone wrong?... Why are they here?"

This was the power of *khaki* uniforms despite the sickly bodies hidden beneath them.

Mr Shastri, sitting on his lawn, was reading the newspaper, which was his only way of filling his time. Otherwise, he never attached any importance to that piece of paper which according to him was blackened uselessly with happenings from around the world, ineffectual for the people of Orchard Street to pay attention to. Some MoU signed between some countries of the world somewhere, some riots somewhere in some distant part of the country...blah blah. Moreover, when his existence was unimportant to the world then how could the happenings of that world be of any importance to him? Tit for tat.

     THE REALIZATION

But the only two reasons that he could find to validate his purchase of this piece of paper, the newspaper daily, despite all his aversions to it, were powerful enough to counter his perspective of it. First was the employment that it would have provided to some people somewhere in the country. And so, he was also contributing his share every month towards this noble cause by paying for that otherwise useless piece of paper, making him earn some good *karma*. Other than this, the most important reason that he loved to boast in front of everybody was that that useless paper was still a better choice than talking to his still more useless wife to fill his time.

But the day the rumbling sound of that heavy motorcycle was heard climbing the steep road to Orchard Street, Mr Shastri was not reading the newspaper, but was merely using it as a shield to hide his face. And that too from Palaram.

On hearing the noise, he put his paper beside the chair and came to the street. Palaram was sitting in a corner, planting seedlings, with his head lowered to such an extent that it disappeared between his legs, making him appear like a bundle from a distance.

Unpleasant happenings of the past are better to be buried down, but in a moment like this when Orchard Street was resonating with the rumbling of that bike, it was impossible to understand the happenings that were going to unfold in the next few moments without digging upon those happenings of the past...a very recent past.... just two hours before that moment.

It was in the morning itself that Palaram had again done something to flare up Mr Shastri's anger. And what Palaram had done could have flared up anybody's anger, especially if that person was obsessed with believing himself to be intelligent and smart, something which Mr Shastri did, and displayed publicly, without ever shying, even at the cost of his wife.

Mrs Shastri, who was fond of maintaining the lawn had been persisting Palaram to plant some flower seedlings from the last few days. Palaram, despite being the scrimshanker that he was, that morning had appeared with a handful of marigold seedlings, really surprising the old lady. Mr Shastri himself was amazed as it was the first time that Palaram had done something on his wife's command, without his intervention. He told Mr Shastri that he had purchased them from the horticulture nursery for fifty rupees, making Mr Shastri pay him back the amount.

"It's all because of my fear that this useless Palaram walked to the horticulture nursery in the town to purchase these seedlings," Mr Shastri bragged in front of his wife. Just an ordinary incident, an insignificant one to find a place in memory. But there might have occurred some disastrous planetary movement in Palaram's horoscope at that moment. The upheaval in the horoscope led to the event that unfolded within two hours after he charged Mr Shastri those fifty rupees.

Palaram was passing his time, as usual, sitting in some corner of the lawn when Ramchand entered Mr Shastri's house on the pretext of conveying a message from Loveena.On finding the bundle of seedlings lying in a corner, he merely said one line and that was the line that had created the whole chaos.

"Sa'ab, tell Palaram to take more seedlings from me if he needs them."

"From you? Why?" Mr Shastri asked in a confused voice.

"I had grown enough seedlings to plant them in our lawn. And when Palaram asked me for some, I gave him these seedlings. But I still have enough. So, if he needs more, he can take them from me."

"Had you charged him any money for these seedlings?" By now Mr Shastri's rising anger had started making him gasp for breath.

"How can I do such a thing sa'ab?" saying this Ramchand, not knowing anything about the incident that had happened that morning, feeling surprised left the place.

     THE REALIZATION

Mr Shastri, on turning his head, found Palaram squeezed into a corner, watching over him.

"Palaram, you useless fellow....," thundered Mr Shastri.

Getting fooled by him, Mr Shastri's ego was badly hurt. This erupted a volcano of anger within him. Walking briskly towards Palaram, Mr Shastri was ready to spring a volley of abuses towards him, when, in a fraction of a second, Mrs Shastri's anticipated reaction if she came to know about it, put a sudden brake on his tongue. The mere thought of Mrs Shastri laughing at him for getting fooled by Palaram was something he dreaded even thinking about. Highly unacceptable. And being fooled by Palaram...highly highly unacceptable. But despite all the unacceptance, he was unable to vent his anger. So, after calming down himself he slowly walked towards Palaram.

"You consider yourself to be very smart. But now you see how difficult it is to... play around with me (how could the words *fool me* be used by Mr Shastri for himself and that also by Palaram... highly and highly unacceptable). I am going to report the matter to the police." Mr Shastri, to balm his injured ego, threatened him but in a *hushed-up* tone.

Still failing to come to terms with the fact of getting fooled by Palaram, and in the absence of any other alternative to vent out that anger, he had opened the newspaper in front of him subsequently feeling more agitated while watching Palaram from the corner of his eyes.

A fuming heart embedded in the body attached to the face hidden beneath that useless, blackened piece of paper and a trembling heart embedded in the body attached to the face hidden in between two legs... both these hearts were jolted out by that heavy sound of the bike climbing up the hill. Police bike...Ah! Why? Mr Shastri came running out onto the road followed by Palaram. Both were stunned. Mr Shastri on anticipating that the police's appearance in Orchard Street had something to do with Palaram and Palaram was trembling with fear assuming that Mr Shastri had reported the matter to the police. Both men glanced at each other.

Before the motorcycle could come to a halt...in the blink of an eye, Palaram jumped onto the road and sprang on Mr Shastri's feet and this unanticipated act of Palaram caught Mr Shastri unawares making him lose his balance. Khatun Begum who was coming out of Loveena's house, getting bewildered on seeing this sequence of events taking place, started shouting in a high-pitched voice.

"Help, help. Palaram has attacked Shastriji. Save him...help...."

With the two police officers struggling to park their heavy bike, residents rushing out of their houses and two men lying flat on the road...the chaotic scene was adequate to panic the weak and feeble-hearted Mrs Shastri, who had come rushing out on hearing hullabaloo outside her house. Failing to understand anything, she started wailing. The whole scene made people believe that Orchard Street had committed its first-ever crime. But why Orchard Street... it could be the first-ever crime in that small town.

"I bet this is just the beginning. Now we should prepare ourselves for hearing more news about crimes in our town."

"I had never ever imagined Palaram to have criminal intentions."

The small crowd surrounding Mr Shastri and Palaram was full of enthusiasm getting something to discuss about, something to lament over and something to fill their bland lives with. Mr Shastri and Palaram were still lying down with their breaths held up -but both had their own reason - Mr Shastri in the fear of getting that incident exposed making him the laughing stock in the locality and Palaram in anticipation of getting cuffed up by the police.

   THE REALIZATION

But the two policemen, after parking their motorcycle a few meters away from that crowd, walked on foot...and silently passed by them without paying any attention to them.

A crime had taken place but not in Orchard Street.

Indira market, the four-storeyed square shopping arcade enclosing a well-manicured lawn in the centre was the heart of the town. The shops existing within the confines of the shopping arcade, catering to the needs of the locals, accounted for the sole reason behind the vivacity of the place. Many small eating joints on the ground floor, with tables laid outside in the lawn, making people enjoy the brightness and warmth of the winter sun or the cool summer breeze under the shade of huge multi- coloured umbrellas while having their food, snacks or drinks was the capital pursuit of the inhabitants to get respite from the monotony of their lives. Harsimran's shop on the second floor, having large glass windows, with the aroma of spices wafting out of it, had the might to attract every passer*by. Lahori masale* scribbled in big bold letters, defining their legacy from a town which they had left behind eighty years back, was still holding on to its magic. Every day was alike in the market complex -sluggish, with slow-paced business going on at the shops -the grocers, greengrocers, tailors, cloth shops, chemists, footwear shop... a few patients sitting outside a small homeopathy clinic. Nobody was in a hurry -only peace and calmness.

Ouch..

A panicked female shriek, steaming the sluggishness, created a furore. The sudden eruption of loud noises vexed the calm of the place. It didn't take long for people to identify the source of that shriek- a middle-aged woman standing near the homeopathic clinic. Something had happened to that woman and the sprinting youth she was pointing towards was the culprit behind that *something*. Without knowing anything else, the people standing nearby had started running behind him. The young perpetrator, running through the passageways of the four-storeyed shopping arcade, was climbing down the stairs in an effort to get rid of them. Coming out of the market complex, standing in front of the police station, panting with fear, and with the small crowd still running behind him, he felt confused for a moment not knowing where to hide. Then he dashed past the police station and the temple, only to escape into a solitary shop in a neglected corner behind the market complex. The heavy aluminum framed doors having brown opaque glasses were now the only shield between that culprit and the huffing-puffing crowd.

What that man had done had never happened there earlier-he had bumped into a woman in the corridor and snatched her gold chain, making her shout at him, thus raising an alarm. This incident took place at nine o'clock in the morning when the shops were still opening up. The head constable had also just unlocked the police station and the ASI had just reached there. The two had not yet properly settled into their seats when the woman whose chain was snatched reached there along with two other men and urged them to accompany them to that shop where the perpetrator was hiding.

"Lodge the complaint and we will investigate it," replied the constable in a casual tone to pacify the complainants.

"But when we know where the chain snatcher is hiding, why are you not interested in coming with us to arrest him?" retorted a bald man, the owner of a footwear shop in the market complex, who was accompanying the victim. Notwithstanding the anger and arguments, the ASI ordered the constable to accompany them to the shop where the culprit was hiding. The place was being guarded by a small crowd. The lack of any signboard indicating the purpose of the shop was making the crowd curious. And so, a portly man, another companion of the complainant, and who was also a shopkeeper, was standing with his face cupped between the

     THE REALIZATION

palms of his hands, closely compressed against the dark opaque glass of the aluminum door to get a glimpse of the things going on inside.

It was with reluctance that the constable slightly pushed open the heavy aluminum door giving sight of the curtain made by sewing together thick gunny bags, whiffing out something scandalous going behind those thick gunny curtains. The constable swayed away the curtain with his baton. The faint yellow of a small bulb was the only source of light in that small hall with its windows tightly secured and covered by thick gunny bag curtains. A shady and dark place, indicating the carrying out of equally shady and dark activities in those premises. The hall with a dozen wooden and plastic chairs arranged in lines indicated it to be a hub of some collective activity. But at that time, they found only two men inside-one telling something to the other who was intermittently scolding him. The appearance of the policeman silenced both.

The constable's unwillingness to enter the place was enough to make the complainants furious, making them almost drag the scrawny policeman inside to carry out a physical search of the culprit. The lanky man with whom the chain snatcher was talking was the owner of the place. A shrewd and relaxed smile on the thin and dry lips of the owner's rawboned face was sufficient to declare his indifference towards the situation. On not recovering the gold chain even after physically searching the perpetrator, the constable heaved a sigh of relief. But the moment the complainants forced him to search the owner, the policeman's face got splashed with the colour of nervousness, making him steal glances towards the owner of the shop, whose smile had now evaporated, leaving behind a stern expression on his face. The series of events that took place made the woman reclaim her gold chain.... from the owner. The furore generated by the incident exposed not only the activities carried out at that shady place but also the relationship of interest between the owner and the policemen. It was a video parlour screening C-grade movies and also indulged in distributing locally brewed alcohol and legally prohibited weed to its customers. The two policemen tried to hush up the incident. And they tried to hush it up because everything was carried out under their patronage in lieu of which they were both paid regularly by the owner.

In a small town like this, the incident being the only one of its kind, it soon came to the notice of the local press. The press and the police station matched only on account of the workforce that they had, otherwise, the press far exceeded the other in its deplorability due to its even more severe financial constraints. The two people who assembled to form the press were -one the owner of that printing press, who was a freelancer doubling as a journalist, editor and distributor, and the other one his employee responsible for the cleaning and maintenance of the place and also for distributing that local newspaper in the town. A small shop on the second floor of the Indira market was the place that served as the press.

A two-page newspaper ...or better to be called a pamphlet carrying the name *Chintan* was its sole publication that used to come out whenever it got its two pages full of some content, finding which was a herculean task for its owner.

With insufficient resources, he was always in dire requirement of funds. His need always kept him hounding out for disturbing news of the town -crimes, corruption...anything. Crime was rare but corruption in government schemes was quite ample. Once he got hold of such news, instead of publishing it, he would use it to blackmail the concerned officers of the authorities, minting out money from them. Following these practices, he was left with enough money to live a comfortable life but no news to publish in *Chintan*, except for news regarding some trivial fight between students at some primary school or regarding some robbery in some distant place or ...any news that was of least interest for the residents. After all, being this compilation of nothing but trash, who

          THE REALIZATION

would have wanted to buy *Chintan*? He published a few hundred copies every few weeks and got them distributed free of cost to the shops in the market complex. This was his way of keeping his terror alive amongst the negative elements of society and *to earn a living*.

It was the first time that he had gotten hold of news about a significant matter that even the two policemen were trying to hush up. He tried to threaten them with the objective of getting some commission in lieu of maintaining silence on the issue, but the involvement of the public had created pressure on the policemen to lodge a complaint regarding the incident. And for the first time, *Chintan* got a piece of news that interested the residents. Its two pages covered under the headlines, '*A big applause for the woman* and *A shady video parlour-An attack on the culture of the hills*'was published and distributed in haste making the incident reach the higher authorities, prompting the policemen to carry out some investigation to save their skin.

It was in relation to this investigation that the policemen had gone to Orchard Street.

But why Orchard Street?

Because the owner of the parlour was the younger son of Ramchand.

Ramchand and Manju had rarely visited their sons since the time they had expressed their displeasure over the way land was distributed between them. Their elder son blamed their father for giving him the less fertile part of the land to favour the younger one while the younger one indicted him of favouring the elder one by giving him a bigger share.

When the siblings were mouthing bitter words then how could their spouses be left behind? They raved even more bitter remarks, not only against each other but also against Ramchand and Manju.

The elderly couple, maintaining their calm, separated themselves completely from the lives of their grown-up married sons, clearing off their lives from the entanglements of the materialistic worldly clutter.

Both the sons excused themselves from visiting their old parents on the pretext of unhappiness in their lives entrusted upon them by their elderly parents. But now, his younger son had got trapped not only in the chain snatching incident but also in the offences of owning a shady place which had become the breeding ground of illegal activities- playing of C grade movies, and distribution of opium, ganja and other drugs and locally brewed liquor. And now when he was stuck in this problem, he was trying to drag Ramchand's name into the controversy in order to save himself. The policemen had summoned Ramchand to the police station, to which he had complied. Manju was perplexed and so was Loveena, who, with time, had now settled into her new life with the elderly couple intricately weaved into the fabric of her life, becoming a family to her.

Loveena was jolted by the incident, but the peace and tranquility of her soul were not. She felt unease, but no anxieties and restlessness. The night before Ramchand had to go to the police station, she kept sitting in her bed through most of the time, anticipating varied possibilities and outcomes of the incident.

"Remarkable are your ways of engaging the human mind in disturbing situations."

Of late she had developed this unique habit of communicating with *life*. It was only in these recondite moments of thoughtfulness that *life* shuns its abstract form only to express itself in something visible, something living, following her like a shadow...something contemporary to her.

"I wonder why you have entangled Ramchand in this mess. Ramchand...with all his simplicity, magnanimity...why?"

     THE REALIZATION

With these incessant thoughts drifting like clouds in her mind, Loveena got out of the quilt and putting on her slippers she came out on the terrace. The chill of the night had a numbing impact on her thoughts. The resplendence of nature illuminating with the tender, silvery touch of the full moon was spellbinding. Tiny dew drops sparkling like silver on the leaves and the petals of the plants and on the railing of the terrace made her imagine them as tiny beads of perspiration oozing out from nature which was calmly indulged in the laborious task of clearing itself off of all the redundancies generated into it by the human mind. Everything was gleaming softly in its purity. She glanced at the stillness of Ramchand's cottage where the couple must be sleeping peacefully.

"This entanglement is not of any significance for Ramchand....but is for you." *Life* whispered sweetly in her ear.

"For me? How...?"

And the *life* exhaled out a soft but chilled gush of air gently stroking the curls of her hair.

The appearance of the policemen in Orchard Street had undoubtedly aroused the curiosity of the residents but not to the same extent as that of Khatun. Everybody including Ramchand knew of the chain snatching incident and of the video parlour and of his son's involvement in it-but that was all that they knew. Khatun, with all her meanderings, picking up a word here and there and supplying it with a little bit of her imagination was the one who claimed to know what others were ignorant of. So, the day Ramchand was summoned to the police station she appeared in Loveena's house, not for her morning chores but with the story behind.

The day had started, maintaining its pace like all other days except for the deep silence prevailing in the house. Despite Manju's persistence to accompany her husband to the police station, he had refused to take her along and Loveena decided it to be more appropriate to wait and watch for the outcome of the situation. So, both the ladies had stayed back. But it didn't take them long to know about why Ramchand had been called to the police station.

"Your son is minting money out of that parlour business." "Settling comfortably at her usual spot near the dining table, Khatun's utterings in her loud and raspy voice were directed at Manju who was working in the kitchen, hearing which she had now come out. Loveena also pulled her chair close to her.

"But he is not alone in all this. He was paying a handsome amount to those worthless policemen for their patronage."

Khatun Begum took a long breath and stopped for a moment to enjoy the awed expression of her audience on being made aware of the sensational information.

"But what is Ramchand's role in all this?"

Anxiety in Loveena's voice accompanied by the blank expression on Manju's face was the desired reaction for Khatun.

"Poor Ramchand...He has no role in it, but they are trying to hush up the issue by getting a statement from him that because of his illness, whose treatment required money, their son was forced into this business. Then the policemen, on emotional grounds, would let him go scot-free."

The devout wife and an ardent believer of her husband's decisions that Manju was, she had never approved of her son's behaviour but had also never imagined that her son could stoop so low that he would take advantage of his own father. The overwhelming pain of her soul bleared her eyes, finding its way out.

"Wretchedness, despondency, ill fate...and many other words arousing sympathy are capable of getting themselves harnessed in the part of the heart which has kept its innocence intact and is full

    THE REALIZATION

of love and compassion. It is this part of the human heart which others easily exploit. When the sins committed are layered with these feelings, they are atoned for sacred, making them pardonable. ...And your son...and the policemen are trying to do the same.... and today Ramchand has been summoned to get his statement of confirmation so as to atone his son's sins."

It was a day when only Khatun spoke....and spoke uninterruptedly. After sitting there for the time, she had designated with to spend at Loveena's house she took their leave.

The day appeared somewhat longer but when Ramchand returned in the evening there was nothing unusual about his facial expressions or his behaviour or mannerism-everything exhibited serenity and peace, devoid of any sign of fear or agitation or helplessness. While this calmed down Loveena's anxieties a bit, it also puzzled her. So, in the evening when she found the elderly couple sitting on a cot outside their outhouse, she also settled herself on a chair lying nearby to talk to them.

"Have you consented to your son's statement?"

Loveena, who since the morning had been hoping that Ramchand would not support his son's statement and would get his son punished for all his acts, suddenly felt a dread in her heart in anticipation of any affirmative response from the old man.

"Nah... why should I?"

"Hmm..." Loveena's deep sigh, clearing her heart of her anticipations, relaxed her.

"You have done the right thing. But aren't you upset with your son?"

Hmm....his deep exhalation was either his admittance or an effort to search for suitable words to put his deep, extraordinary and meaningful thoughts in. Loveena failed to understand.

"Life and its relations keep on evolving. There was a time when my children were young and completely dependent upon us for their survival. We, without knowing the ultimate outcome of our upbringing, tried to nurture them with the best of what we possessed. As they grew up, our relations also grew and attained maturity. When a relation attains maturity nothing more is left to give to that relation. I gave them all that I possessed, but without knowing how much they had imbibed up my efforts."

Ramchand's gravelly voice overflowing with calmness and wisdom diffused into the surroundings, giving an illusion of this wisdom expanding in every direction in the quietness of the night. His words seemed to be giving a new dimension to Loveena's thoughts. Loveena, who earlier had always believed in the intactness of relations, had never thought about this aspect. But now, with Ramchand's words, she was visualizing their growth, the changing shapes and colours of all her relations, ultimately leading to their maturity, finally splitting open up to expose the hidden seeds. Seeds which are analogous to grown-up children or adults, ready to undergo that cycle again. After letting go of the seeds, was it still possible to exercise any control over them? Neither it is possible, nor is there any necessity to do it. Ah! words inducing realization... the ultimate realization.

"With myself getting fully drenched, fully satisfied in the role of a father, I had moved off the field long back by withdrawing all my fatherly attributes. Now I am their well-wisher. But the responsibility to make choices in life is theirs and theirs alone. If one understands and accepts this ever-evolving face of relations, then nothing to fear is left behind, there is nothing to get upset about. Why should I feel anxious? Now it is time for them to drench themselves in this worldly ocean to understand it...and that is possible only if they want to understand it. But I know that they are sinking deeply into the illusions of this *samsara,* in a race to grab more and more. It

  THE REALIZATION

is either their will or their destiny. Whatever it may be, I have no role to play in it."

Manju, besides being a wife and a mother, was also an ardent believer of what Ramchand was saying. And so, in moments like these when Ramchand, lost in his thoughts, poured out his accumulated wisdom, she sat silently with her hands lying in her lap and gaze fixed on snow-capped mountains.

"It is not only relation with our children that gains maturity, but all our worldly relations. Just like my relationship with my wife Manju."

On the mention of Manju's name, both Manju and Loveena felt equally surprised.

"The both of us, with our respective traits, have filled in the hollowness in each other's lives." A faint smile played on Ramchand's thin lips making Manju lower her wrinkled face.

"But don't you think that the relations are a fountainhead of miseries?" Loveena's doubts had found their way out in the form of words.

"Hmm...Nah." Ramchand's monosyllable weighed down with his laboured breathing of old age, was not followed by anything for a few moments, as if to give her time to push down the accumulated words of wisdom spoken till now into the depths of her soul.

"Nah... diversity in relations is the only meaningful thing in this world. Diversity is a thing to aspire for. Whether the diversity is in nature or relations...it only brings enrichment along with it."

"Diversity of relations...yes, I also have experienced it-each having a different texture, different taste..." With the thoughts, in a moment, Loveena's whole life, her parents, grandparents, Babli, Sanand, Vikram... everything flashed before her eyes.

"The experiences from these multifarious relations are a prerequisite to shatter worldly illusions of the restive human mind. With the wiping away of these illusions, the restiveness also gets wiped away, leaving behind a peaceful mind...in tandem with the ever-peaceful soul. A peaceful mind and peaceful soul- the pinnacle of satisfaction and the only objective of this journey of life, but something that very few are able to attain. Once this objective is reached, no desire to have anything else is left. And it is only when this satisfaction is experienced that the flower of detachment blooms."

The divinity of the moment, sweetened with the nectar of the old man's words of wisdom, was trickling down deep into the depths of Loveena's soul while dissolving the leftovers of restiveness from her mind.

"A dissatisfied heart, with its yearnings, can only experience frustration towards or aversion from this world, whereas only satisfaction can lead to detachment-detachment from everything or in other words oneness with everything- oneness full of love. With this detachment one gets attached to the whole- this beautiful and mysterious *samsara* and its creator, vanishing all feelings of drudgery, pain, hatred...leaving behind only love. Then the pleasure of diving into that huge ocean of love is indescribable." Ramchand concluded leaving Loveena pondering over his every word, memorizing it till eternity.

That night, sitting in the coziness of her room on the terrace, in front of the *bukhari* glowing with the warmth of red-hot coals burning inside it, Ramchand's words were the only thing which occupied her mind.

Allow yourself to be drenched completely into this samsara to learn its ways Ramchand's words reverberated in her ears.

How wrong had she been!

The youth that she had spent in an overcrowded city provided her with so many opportunities to be a part of that crowd but the deficit of faith that she was implanted with deterred her from doing so. When she found herself surrounded by people in her school and in the university-people gossiping, laughing or rushing past brushing against her, even then she never felt a desire to connect with any one of them. But now, living in the scantily inhabited locality of the hills, she had allowed herself to get drenched by the ways of life so as to be a part of that *samsara* again.

There come certain moments in life that make one ponder over one's naivety in experiencing the manifoldness of relations during life's journey, devoiding him of the joys and the purpose of living. The aloofness which was made to be a part of her character had crushed all her desires to experience that diversity and how erroneous that had been.

The luminous silvery moon, clearly visible through the full-length glass window of her room was suffusing the darkness with its brimful glory. With an intent gaze fixed on it for a long time, it started giving her the illusion of a hole in the veil of the dark night sky. The hole, which was giving a glimpse of brightness on the other side of that dark veil. This grand journey of life is undertaken only for lifting or understanding this darkness so as to emerge on that other side, the side, which is fully illuminated with that soothing, healing silvery brilliance.

THE SEEKER

*B*looming of peace and joy in life had started perfecting Loveena's sensory reflexes. During her routine evening walks along the steep mountainous trails, even the slightest changes in the surroundings had now started becoming noticeable to her, something she herself was amazed at.

The expansive wilderness unrolled all around seemed to rest in a peaceful state, protected by magnificent snow-capped mountains on all sides. With this intriguing beauty all around, but visible only for those few who can relish it, who are able to imbibe it into their soul and are truly deserving. The steep trails scattered throughout the place seemed like a trial laid down by the mountains to pick out only the deserving seekers. Only those who are desired by the mountains dare to even tread them. These are the ones to whom the mountains want to disclose the mysteries of life, of the world, of this *samsara*. And then those who succeed in understanding the language of the mountains and nature become immune to the trivialities of *samsara*, always delving into bliss.

Loveena, with all her yearnings, was probably amongst one of those seekers who were embraced by the mountains, and a well-deserving one at that. She started deciphering the language of nature, sensing the breath of every creation all around her. Whenever a new seedling germinated, or a flower bloomed, she smelled the change by inhaling the aroma of the place. She sensed the clouds long before they became visible from behind those mountains by feeling the texture of the moisture-laden air against her skin. The appearance of new flocks of birds on the horizon indicated to her the upcoming change in weather. She had instinctively started acknowledging every change in nature. On her way she whispered to every plant, every tree, every bird, everything...and they all had also started responding to her. She had now started sensing their breaths and whispers while passing by them.

Rarely did she encounter anybody on those trails, but whenever she did, she felt that person to be different from the rest of world. The difference lay not in their anatomy, but in their *aura*, in the spirit which they imbued into their surroundings. Those were the people who never seemed to be in a hurry to reach their destination and were usually immersed in themselves. The more she noticed, the more she learned. And the more she learned, the more joyful she felt. This exhilaration started settling down all her scores with life, making her friends with it.

A rare friendship.

Senses manifest themselves in the form of desires which are nothing but the traps for worldly entanglements, leading to frustrations and weariness of the soul. But the heightening of the senses grants them the penetrability to perceive the abundance of life hidden beyond worldly illusions, thus settling the doubts of the mind. Then the manifestation of these senses and desires are in tandem with the whisperings of the soul.

One such desire...or the whispering of the soul that Loveena acknowledged was what made her interact with the young ascetic she had encountered during one of her walks. He was on his way down from somewhere in those mountains. On her way, she had encountered a few people earlier also, but it was the first time that she had felt the urge to talk to them.

The dense forest, with its towering pine trees so dense that komorebi formed on the damp forest floor densely scattered with pine needles, was quite enchanting. The slight cool breeze delicately touching the branches of the trees was busy changing the patterns of the dappled sunlight on the forest floor.

A young ascetic with ragged orange garb wrapped around his slender frame was taking a rest under a tree. His face, from a distance, with his long black hair tied into a big bun resting on his head and his face covered beneath a dense black beard, was giving an illusion of a bundle of hair lying on top of a body. On a closer look, the only part of his face visible was his furrowed forehead, which was also smeared with sandalwood paste. A small sack of his belongings was lying beside him.

On coming across a well-dressed middle-aged lady at such an unlikely place seemed to catch him by surprise, which was visible in the curiosity of his eyes. After exchanging greetings, she sat on a small rock lying across the place where he was resting.

"*Baba*, where are you coming from?"

He pointed towards the snow-clad mountains.

"From the abode of Lord Shiva?"

"Hmm...," the overstretched monosyllable he uttered seemed to be a prelude to some more profound insights to Loveena, contrary to which it was followed by a long silence.

"Can you tell me more about life in the mountains?"

Long since her conversations with Ramchand and Manju, Loveena had always harboured in her a desire to know something more about those snow-clad mountains, the existence of life in the caves somewhere over there...and so many other things.

"The people of the world can never understand our lives. We live in caves, devoid of all the comforts of home, to conquer our

    THE SEEKER

senses…. Huh," inhaling and then exhaling a deep breath as if vexed with the question, he finished his sentence "…our sole intent is to understand *samsara* and its mysteries."

"What should be done to gain that understanding?"

It was probably the first time for that young ascetic that anybody had shown any interest in the wisdom that he thought he was in possession of. Buoyed by this feeling of being important, his lips, hidden beneath his thick matted beard, broke into a simpered smile.

"It is a very difficult path…very difficult and people of the world could not understand that."

He took a long pause in the hope of getting prodded by the elderly lady, making him feel more important. But on not getting the desired response he resumed his talk.

"We numb our senses by exposing ourselves to the chilling cold of the snow-covered mountains, by devoiding ourselves of food and water for many days, by not speaking anything except for chanting His name and by not listening to anything except for His name… We numb our senses till we stop feeling their existence. It is a very tough *sadhana*."

"What do you achieve after enduring such suffering?"

"God…It is only after being successful in this *sadhana* that one can attain *moksha*, liberation from repeated cycles of birth and death."

"Have you succeeded?"

"It is too early for me, but I am on my way. My master, under whose guidance I am following this *sadhana,* has succeeded in it."

His voice was laced with naive enthusiasm.

"But could you tell me the reason why have you taken this path, the path of abandonment?"

"Because there is nothing worthwhile in this world to spend...or more rightly to waste one's life for."

The earlier enthusiasm of his voice gave way to hidden discontentment and frustrations. After sitting silently for some time, with his gaze fixed on the changing patterns of sunlight on the forest floor, he seemed to be lost in his thoughts. He was battling hard to get hold of that edge of the thread of the story of his life from where he could start telling his story.

"I completed my graduation but failed to get any job. My father, with all his grumblings directed towards me for not providing my family with any financial support, was driving me crazy. My mother's illness, my elder sister's marriage, my younger brother's involvement with ruffian boys...everything, everything made me feel helpless. So, I decided to follow a path which could take me away from the sufferings of the world and can help me in making peace with myself."

Loveena's gaze fixed on that young ascetic, who now seemed to her just an ordinary young boy with all his sufferings, was not seeing him but was seeing through him...her own past. A past when she had also endured that restlessness, those sufferings. Travelling down her memory lane, she struck an instant chord with the state of mind that that young ascetic was now in. She had passed through that phase which the ascetic was passing through now, a long time back. *And it is this understanding which makes one more humane, more compassionate.*

"Hmm....peace with oneself. Yes. That's the most important thing in this world. And without it, every day resembles a hot pot in which the body is burning without getting any respite. Every day resembles an uphill task."

Loveena, immersed in her own experiences from her past, realized that the young ascetic was also on a journey similar to hers.

"...To make peace with self," she again muttered in a soft whisper barely audible to her own ears.

"Have you ever experienced that peace?" Straightening her back against the tree Loveena, in her effort to understand the path of abandonment, volleyed another question towards the ascetic.

Loveena's genuine words, devoid of any judgment, relaxed the young man, making him ponder over the efforts he was putting in to attain that peace. And the truth that one wants to forget, to ignore is always kept neatly folded under the layers of illusions deep down in one's heart, in one's soul...or wherever but very deep inside. It is so deep that if one tries to bring it out then it would devastate the very foundation of the illusions built over it. So, a lot of effort is required to bring that truth out in the open. And that young man was also battling with that effort.

"Nah," after taking a long time, it seemed he had been drained of all his courage in uttering that single word. He mumbled with his gaze fixed somewhere on the horizon.

"I don't know what peace is. From the day I left my family, I have merely been wandering in an effort to justify my act of escaping from my duties, of protecting myself from the miseries of life by avoiding them."

Loveena, sitting silently, was listening intently to the words uttered by him. And being a good listener, she not only listened but felt the pain and despair hidden beneath his words.

"I have abandoned everything and followed all the *sadhana* as directed by my master, have tried to numb my senses to gain *moksha*...but the moment I stop chanting, my inner voices start lamenting me, the moment I close my eyes I visualize my mother's suffering, the moment I stop listening to the chantings I start hearing lamentations of my father...so everything that I am doing to make peace with myself seems futile."

The truth which he was unable to accept was now in the open, devastating him, demolishing the palace of illusion he had built within, to deceive himself that he had left everything for some bigger cause- the cause of merging with Him, to make peace with himself. But after wandering here and there, now, sitting in front of a middle-aged woman he was admitting the very truth he was trying to escape from, with his tears streaming down his eyes getting lost somewhere in that matted beard, resembling raindrops falling down getting absorbed by dried and caked up soil.

"Hmm…Nothing is futile in this world." After a long silence, Loveena, still lost in her thoughts uttered her first sentence.

"Don't belittle your efforts," Loveena's comforting voice stopped the stream of tears rolling down his eyes giving way to hope.

"You have already realized that you need to make peace with yourself. Don't you think that this realization lays down the very foundation of all the efforts you are going to put in that direction? This realization in itself is a big achievement, a steppingstone for changing the course of life."

Loveena's words started making sense to the young man and this was reflected in the placidity with which he was listening to her without even blinking his eyes.

"You know what you want and now the only dilemma confusing you is –how. How can that peace be attained? Hmm…I myself have gone through a phase of restlessness and I was not even aware of the fact that this restlessness could be settled only by making *peace with myself.* I was searching for it outside. So, I started on a journey in search of solitude, of peace. But it was the words of Ramchand which made me realize that all this restlessness arises from within. This restlessness crushes all the peace and joys of life we are born with. This restlessness is not because of our senses but by the corruption of these senses by the negativities arising out of our thoughts. So, don't try to numb your senses but utilize them in seeing and feeling the purity scattered all around you. Try to decipher the language of silence, the language of these magnificent trees, of those snow-clad mountains, the sound of the running stream of water...you will sense the joys and pleasures scattered all around you, satiating your senses, settling all your inner chaos. And then, peace would itself bless you."

"Is Ramchand your *guru*?"

"Guru!?"

The young man's question left Loveena pondering over her thoughts.

*"Guru...*Hmm..." She suddenly felt amazed at the question because earlier she had never given it a thought. And in a fraction of a second faces of Ramchand, the mystic at the temple...everything floated before her eyes.

"Yes...you can say so. Everybody who gives direction to life or makes you understand it properly is a *guru*...this forest is also my *guru*."

In the deep silence of the forest, stirred occasionally by the chirping of birds, the middle-aged woman and the young ascetic, both sat immersed in their own thoughts for a long time. Loveena's words uttered in her soft voice, filled the eyes of the young man with optimism.

"You have also given me a glimpse into the miseries and pains embedded in the hearts of the people, who after renouncing this world, are living in the caves of the snow-covered mountains. It means the source of miseries and pains is within and not outside in this world." Loveena voiced out her sudden realization.

"Never think that you are the only one struggling with this feeling. Every person on this earth undergoes the same feelings, the same emotions at one time or the other. The reasons for their inner turmoil may vary but the turmoil is always there in the human mind. So, who would not like to settle that restlessness, that turmoil? But everybody's efforts to settle that chaos are different."

Life's magnanimity is hard to decipher -the magnanimity which lies in the subtlety with which it adapts itself to the role of a teacher and a seeker simultaneously. The flow of wisdom between the two seekers at that moment was two-way. While teaching one another both were simultaneously learning also. The young ascetic unknowingly had made Loveena dig into that lone corner of her heart which she herself had also evaded for a long time. That lone corner which still kept on emanating puffs of smoke in her soul creating occasional stirs and restlessness inside her.

THE SEEKER

A VISIT

*M*any days... many weeks had passed since Loveena's meeting with that young ascetic.

Whenever some decision, which the heart always tried to avoid pondering about, has to be taken, then the count of time loses track. So now, when she had courageously or more aptly... accidentally acknowledged the existence of such a dilemma hidden in an unattended corner inside her heart, she had decided to settle that score also. And that was about her relationship with Vikram. Though that relationship had been quite short-lived, it was also a truth of her life that kept weighing down on her.

"Getting entangled again?" *Life* whispered.

"With whom?" Loveena beamed.

"With me. *In me.*" It whispered back bemusingly.

"Haha....you are a dear friend. How could you, with all your simplicity, entangle anybody? The human mind, with all the thoughts it churns out, is enough for its entanglements, while you with your magnanimity and omnipresence have distributed yourself amongst us- all the living beings. Isn't it nothing but our illusion to think that you are entangling us? But isn't the truth that you have already surrendered yourself completely to the will of the human mind?"

❖

When she was approaching that state of bliss- the state she was born with, there still remained some minor tasks on her part that needed to be accomplished.

Vikram's pleadings resonating with his miseries were the reason making her postpone any further encounters with him. In his occasional phone calls to her, he used to bemoan how his children held him responsible for the sufferings of their lives, how they had left him for their mother and how he was living all alone now. In his pleadings, she discerned the feelings of despair and restlessness which she herself had endured and which had made her abandon everything in search of solitude. She was now aware of the fact that every phase of life had a threshold, a climax which when attained made a person cross it over to go into the next phase. The turbulence of relations at Vikram's place was the threshold of the phase when she had shunned everything to cross over into this next phase of her life. And now, her meeting the young ascetic had pushed her towards a threshold again- a threshold to jump into that phase of life which is devoid of all the remnants of confusions of her heart and mind- confusions which had been making her avoid Vikram. So, she had decided to go back to that very place from where she had once run away with all her frustrations a long time back.

"I am all alone, a lonely old man in this house."

Vikram's worn-out face with his slackened skin folding into creases that had now gained permanence in the form of wrinkles, was enough to clearly express the mental agony he was enduring.

"Nobody is ever alone. Everyone has baggage of some sufferings, guilt, desires or something else with him that keeps weighing him down. So, you too are not alone, you are alone with your *baggage*. Sort out that baggage and then you will truly be alone and will be

     A VISIT

amazed at exploring the peace and tranquility that that loneliness has a treasure of."

Vikram's sunken eyes behind his glasses were staring at her without blinking. Loveena noticed a glint of curiosity in those eyes.

"How?"

"How...how could I tell you that? It is everyone's own journey. But I can only tell you that you have to search inside yourself to find out the reasons for your desperations and have to try to settle them down so as to make peace with yourself. With the settling down of the reasons for your chaos, all the chaos will disappear, thus bringing your life in order. It is only then that you will find your life to be a journey that you will be able to cherish."

Taking a long breath, as if trying to read Vikram's mind, Loveena continued, "The sole reasons for your frustrations might be all the happenings which have taken place between you and your family. So, mend those broken relations, nurture them and wait for them to get healed."

"What about my relationship with you?"

"Oh! It was after the passing of my parents, passing through which phase I used to feel that I was left all alone in this world. It was at that time that I rushed into a relationship that I was not carved out for with you, without giving a deep thought to it. Till now, I kept on running away from it. But after that, I have also learned a lot that has made me realize all those things that I have told you now. And now to make complete peace with myself I am here, sitting in front of you facing you."

Loveena's eyes were fixated on infinity and her voice was filled with calmness and serenity reflecting the state of her mind.

"And I don't think that our relationship has anything to do with the despairs of life that you are experiencing now."

The layers of confusion were peeling down revealing the freshness of soul.

"Life's journey is an uphill task with the carriage of all our baggage attached to it. How can one cherish that journey with all the panting while dragging this baggage uphill?"

Resting his slightly stooped shoulders against the back of the sofa, the brightening of his mood reflecting in his voice was noticeable to Loveena, making her relaxed.

''Hmm...who told you Vikram that life is an uphill journey and you yourself are responsible for pulling it upwards? Wouldn't it be more appropriate to consider it a downhill journey with the carriage of baggage attached pushing us down that slide? One neither has the option nor the time to stand still even for a moment. So, one doesn't have any choice except to surrender completely to this whirlwind journey and to just enjoy the gush of air on one's face. So, whether you accept it or not, life is a downhill slide. So, enjoy the slide."

"Haha......"

Vikram was himself amazed by that ringing sound of his laughter. He must have laughed after.... god knows how much time. Suddenly life posed itself in a rainbow of colours in front of his eyes- a rainbow that is formed with a bright sun coming out after a heavy downpour making the surroundings poetic.

"Thanks, Loveena."

"It was nothing that I have done for you. It is something that I am doing for myself to complete all the chapters which I had ever left incomplete in the book of my life."

And with this, Loveena felt as if she had nailed down the last nail in the coffin of her despair.

    A VISIT

END OF THE WORLDLY MORASS

Repudiation of the ticking of the clock, of the slipping away of years and of the existence of fears is enough to fill the chasms of life with tranquility- the only prerequisite to taste the supreme elixir of life which is the sole axle of its journey. The fine layers of time slither away revealing the changing circumstances, changing perspectives, changing seasons... If *time* is worldly then the sublimities concealed under it are *divine*. These revelations, when acknowledged by the human mind lead to the heightening of senses, thus enabling them to delve into those changes making them relish it. Then the seasons do not remain mere phases of a year but become the grandest gift of the creator to be relished and admired. And human existence starts reveling in the sensations aroused by their delicate touch against the skin, seeping in its smoothness like a sponge. Ah...the perfection with which every change is crafted becomes a thing to marvel about. Then the varied forms of emotions start melting into one another, fusing together, nullifying each other, leaving behind a void, a vacuum, making one completely detached from everything, thus tearing through the veil of worldly illusions, to finally give a glimpse of the oneness of the whole creation beneath it...*the supreme axle of the grand creation.*

The beauty in the fluttering of birds, in the ruffling of dried-up leaves, in the fragrance and colours of vegetation, in the gentle blowing of breeze, in the fierceness of storms.... can finally be deciphered.

The universe and the soul start reverberating in unison and nature starts communicating with the soul, opening up its treasures of wisdom to the human mind leading to the culmination of life in a blissful way.

Loveena failed to notice when the black of her hair attained the softness of white and the sheen of her youthful skin slowly got hidden under fine lines of her slackened skin. And she also failed to notice when the restlessness of her soul got lost in the serenity and tranquility she had now achieved, which was now oozing out in the form of exuberance. She failed to notice when every day, despite its usual ordinariness, had started revealing its newness to her.

How could all the days be the same, when every day takes a bit of youth with it, which is noticeable, but also leaves behind a part of itself, leaving one to introspect it, to search for its meaning? Loveena had failed on many accounts only to be successful in this introspection.

Her walks through the woods soothed her soul. Dense forests of pine trees blessed with evergreen needles, with synchronicity in their height, in the straightness of the manner in which they grow made her forget to blink her eyes. Sitting by the stream under those trees, while delving into the depths of the crystal blue of the slowly moving stream, she often became unaware of the mellowing down of the bright yellow of the sun into soft orange. Occasionally she experienced a sense of oneness between her inner energy and the energy of her surroundings, startled by the flow of the current that would set in between them. She felt connected with every tree, shrub, grass...everything.

      END OF THE WORLDLY MORASS

The rumbling, jumbling stream of water arising somewhere in the ice-capped mountains, the *abode of Lord Shiva,* shone like gold under the yellow of the bright afternoon sun. White foam formed at the spot where the stream touched the ground after leaving the magnificent heights of the mountains. This whole event, to her, analogized itself to human life, where the falling down of the stream is comparable to birth leading to the separation of both the stream and the soul from their source, their creator and the dismay appearing in the form of froth in water and in the form of restlessness in the soul. Unlike that divine stream which soon gets rid of that froth by abandoning it, the restlessness of the soul keeps pumping itself up, filling every pore of the human body. It is only when the soul gets itself rid of that froth of restlessness that it can undertake its further journey with the calmness of that stream.

With passing years, her sitting at that spot by the stream had become a ritual for her, and the gradual easing out of the restlessness of her soul had started reflecting in the stillness of her posture. The more still she became, the more she started deciphering the sounds of nature, thus developing a sense of kinship with it.

Loveena, sitting on the thick bed of dried-up needles under the pine tree, was inhaling deeply the invigorating summer breeze overladen with the coolness borrowed from the melting ice of the mountains. With her back resting against the trunk of the pine tree, she sensed a delicate and comforting pat on her shoulder.

"Your height is mesmerizing." She whispered under her breath, "It motivates humans to attain the pinnacle of name and fame."

The sudden gush of cool breeze slightly swayed the magnificent tree as if in acknowledgement. Hahaha....laughed the pine tree, "You have seen my height but not the confinement. My height motivates humans to achieve name and fame, but doesn't my confinement teach you anything?"

"What?" The divulgence was unthought of for Loveena, making her confused.

"To confine the desires, to limit them. Otherwise, their rampant growth will suck out all the joys of life." Chuckled the pine tree.

"Confinement of desires...Ah! So true."

The vastness of the clear blue sky, with the orange ball of setting sun hugged to its bosom and white cotton balls of clouds playing hide and seek in its lap, caught hold of her attention. With the expanse of that clear blue vastness all around her, she imagined as if every existence on the earth was tenderly and securely enveloped in that vastness. She uttered dreamily, "Your vastness is captivating."

"Hmm..." the sky whispered back, "My vastness captivates you, but what about my emptiness, my purity?"

Loveena felt hypnotized brooding over each and every word.

"You appreciate my vastness but do not want to empty yourself of all the grudges, dishonesty...negativities that you harbour inside you. I never hold back anything in myself. It is my beauty, my purity that shines back in the blue of my colour, in the brightness of the sun and the twinkling of stars in the darkness of night. So, empty yourself of all the grudges by forgiveness and find out that vastness within."

"Forgiveness...," she murmured and felt as if she was still struggling to accommodate this word in her life.

"Isn't acceptance the better way than forgiving or forgetting?"

"Ah...don't get yourself trapped in words. Forgiveness or forgetting or acceptance...all have the same essence- letting nothing waver you."

The words of wisdom from the sun made her retrospect her life. Slowly closing her eyes, she let herself drift to that part of consciousness where she was merely reduced to a spectator of

     END OF THE WORLDLY MORASS

her own worldly life, with no strings attached to any incident unfolding in front of her eyes. Every character displayed itself in the form of thoughts, and she was horrified on witnessing a massive combat taking place between them, making them more distorted, scarier. The thoughts that dazzled her eyes were the ones which had retained their purity and divinity intact. She pitied how those were also dragged into that combat, corrupting their purity and for which they will have to undergo a long struggle throughout life to acquire it again.

The memories of her childhood played before her eyes when her father used to narrate to her the stories from past generations when bloody massacres were carried out at different places on earth and to keep whose memory alive, monuments had been built in those places. In the light of wisdom gained now, she pondered over the futility of all these efforts. When the earth is struggling to accommodate the ever-growing population, having no place for even the living, then why preserve places of hatred? When it is advised to forgive everyone so as to attain peace of mind and to unleash the vastness of the soul, then why to keep the memories of hatred alive?

She sat flabbergasted on acknowledging the echo of her soul that how the raking up of past events and conflicts, by adding so many new perspectives and new dimensions, which the people of that era might not have even thought of themselves, would help in our betterment? No....recalling hurtful memories can only create revengeful thoughts, capable only of stealing away inner peace.

So why remember what we were rather than what we can be?

When *forgiveness* is the heart of every religion, of every teaching, and is the eternal truth illuminating in the core of the brilliance of the soul and the universe then why keep on clinging to unpleasant memories of the past, castigating the present?

Forgiveness- a word she had listened to umpteen times and had also uttered many more times, she could now feel reverberating all around her, revealing the divinity hidden beneath and invoking a sense of mysticism in her. The faces of her father, her mother, Sanand, Vikram, Babli....and even her own face- all started taking shape in front of her eyes, only to merge with one another, giving her a glimpse of the oneness of the journey of every soul, where everyone is undergoing the same dilemmas and same pains. When there is oneness between them, what is the reason to harbour grudges against each other? In an instant, the massive combat taking place before her eyes came to an abrupt end, with every character and every thought mingling into one, giving her a glimpse of the grand oneness, thus dazzling her eyes with the brilliance of divinity.

The chirping of birds around her brought her out of her stupor and she opened her eyes with a gentle smile on her lips. A flock of birds that seemed to be returning to its shelter at sunset was flying over her.

Ah...sighed Loveena.

"They are so lucky."

"Who?"

"The birds...they can touch you. Only if I had wings...I would then come up to you..." quipped Loveena to the sky.

"Hmm...you are seeing their flight but not their detachment. It is only when they detached themselves from the earthly possessions that they were able to touch me." Smiled the sky.

The pine trees, the sky, the stream...the whole of nature seemed to be smiling at Loveena at that moment.

A slight gush of air ruffled the dried-up leaves touching her feet and then climbed up the heights of the pine trees, delicately swaying their branches. And she got mesmerized by the humility with which

     END OF THE WORLDLY MORASS

that gush of air tickled everything alike without any arrogance of the imperium it was the owner of.

Not sensing the numbness of her limbs caused by the stillness of her posture, sitting on that thick bed of dried-up needles pricking into her skin, she felt an overwhelming joy- a feeling of liberation, of the rainbow of colours all around her- a feeling which can only be felt but can never be explained.

Stones perish to form soil in which grow the plants to give you a fruit which when consumed will become a part of you. Similarly, one day you will perish and some of my seeds will germinate in your ashes only to grow into huge pine trees touching the vastness of the sky. So, we all are one.

In that moment she sensed a fine music arising out from the mountains, the *abode of Lord Shiva.*

Journey to an expanded self awareness

The book opens in the present-day scenario, where a rather unsure Loveena of mid-thirties is boarding a train to Pathankot. Her already raw senses are over burdened by the onslaught of experience of a train station environment. Yet her insecurities are deep seated in her psyche and are result of the generational trauma she endured during her growing up years by the hands of her equally tormented mother Neena, reviews **DEEPAK KUMAR JHA**

The ("Dreamcatcher") is the story of Loveena, the protagonist of the book who is a sensitive soul. It beautifully narrates the journey through her trials and tribulations, her pains and realisations, her metamorphosis and an ultimate 'coming of age' which leaves her in a state of expanded awareness of self as well as her surroundings and people there in. Author Monika has orchestrated her sound knowledge of literature, language and the subject & object to bring on paper the story of a child Loveena, till she finds solace passing through life's labyrinth, unfortunately all nurtured in close walls of her family. The just published book revolves around Loveena's mother Neena who attained motherhood through Loveena after a long wait of ten years. Neena's intensity thus shifted to being extra protective about her daughter from the negativities of the world. Having brought up in a rather affluent and rich family, she desires nothing less for her daughter. And even though Loveena had both her parents-Neena and her father Dev, it was her mother and mother's stories which were to carve her life and make her the person that she would become. And the story's trajectory thus turns to Loveena's mother Neena's life.

Neena's husband Dev was a victim of his own sense of helplessness for his lack of understanding the business of Neena's father and inability to take it up for posterity, even though he was the sole son-in-law the family had. His job as an assistant professor of history in the university projected him as most suitable boy for Neena, when a friend of Neena's father told him about Dev and his docile nature. Quite obviously Neena's father believed it to be the significant trait suitable for her pampered daughter. As Neena entered Dev's life and his house after her wedding, it was bustling with Dev's family. Neena was immediately overwhelmed by the sheer number of people and was unable to adjust to this new environment which was totally unlike her solitary and exclusive upbringing in an affluent household. Sensing Neena's hesitation and reservations, Dev's family too accepted her into their family but without completely absorbing her into their lives. So, even though Neena was married into Dev's family she could never truly become a part of it Dev's detachment or lack of desire to correct this situation further acerbated the relationships. Troubled relations with in-laws, Dev's indifference clubbed with an anguishing wait of ten years to attain motherhood further fed Neena's sense of mistrust and suspicions and her belief that the world was a dangerously bad place. Loveena who was born as a happy child with a calm, pleasing, innocent disposition was always eager to embrace everybody, never earned approval for her behaviour from her mother. Neena always dismissed these traits as incompatible with the ways of world. Thus, growing up, Loveena's world protected by her mother, remained confined within the four walls of the palatial house with the house help Babli as a constant companion who too gets married leaving behind a void in Loveena's life.

Finally, Loveena finds her suitor in Sanand and her engagement to him was greeted as the most welcome news by everyone later on which did not worked due to triggers of Neena's fears. For Loveena this incident proved to be the one which augmented her belief in Neena's words that world is a bad place. Her father Dev too gone followed by passing of Neena. Loveena finally married, not to start a family but only to drown the haunting hollowness of her soul into joys and laughter. Vikram was a colleague of Loveena and the only thing she knew about him was that he was a divorcee with two grown up kids. Soon this too developed a marital conflict. Unable to handle this situation any longer Loveena decides that she needs to get respite from her choppy life that and decides to leave the house and Vikram. She goes looking for solitude in a place away from the chaos of the city, away from the prodding eyes of the society. Her life's journey takes a new turn as she arrives at Pathankot where she embarks upon a spiritualistic journey. Armed with the strength of her soul and her renewed faith in life and self and the world in general, Loveena finally finds herself ready to go back to place from where she herself had once run away from all her life challenges a long time back. Her tumultuous relationship with Vikram's place was when she had shunned everything to cross over into next phase of her life. She was now ready to go meet Vikram as a new person. But this time she isn't running away. This time she is running towards meeting life head-on.

DREAMCATCHER

Author:
Monika Singla

Publisher:
Lithouse
lithousehv@gmail.com

Price: ₹275

Sources: Sunday Pioneer

Sunday, June 30, 2024